KU-110-522

EFFECTIVE SPEECH

Including Public Speaking, Mental Training and the Development of Personality

A COMPLETE COURSE

BY

Dwight E. Watkins, A. M.

ASSOCIATE PROFESSOR OF PUBLIC SPEAKING, UNIVERSITY OF CALIFORNIA; INSTRUCTOR OF PUBLIC SPEAKING, SAN FRANCISCO SALES MANAGERS ASSOCIATION, SAN FRANCISCO STOCK AND BOND EXCHANGE, SAN FRANCISCO CHAPTER AMERICAN INSTITUTE OF BANKING, AND PACIFIC GAS AND ELECTRIC COMPANY; FORMERLY CHAIRMAN ORAL ENGLISH SECTION, NATIONAL ASSOCIATION OF ENGLISH TEACHERS; DIRECTOR OF NATIONAL SPEECH ARTS ASSOCIATION; AUTHOR OF "PUBLIC SPEAKING FOR HIGH SCHOOLS", "THE FORUM OF DEMOCRACY", AND "POEMS FOR ORAL INTERPRETATION."

In Collaboration With

Herbert F. de Bower, LL.B.

AUTHOR OF "ADVERTISING PRINCIPLES", "THE ART OF SALESMANSHIP"; FORMER COMMISSIONER OF CONCILIATION, DEPARTMENT OF LABOR; FOUNDER OF AMERICAN CORRESPONDENCE SCHOOL OF LAW AND ALEXANDER HAMILTON INSTITUTE

VOLUME 1

MANUAL I and II

MARKUS-CAMPBELL COMPANY

CHICAGO, U.S.A.

1948 Edition

Manufactured in the United States of America

PREFACE

A young man came to an old railroad engineer, asking advice as to how to succeed in life.

The grey-haired veteran of the rails eyed his questioner speculatively before saying slowly,

"Son, did you ever see a locomotive engineer watching for signals BEHIND him?"

"Certainly not," came the quick reply.

"Well, son, running a life is much like running a train. You don't want to look for signals behind you. They have or have not served their purpose, but you must keep a keen lookout for signals ahead if you expect to take your 'Old Betsy' into the round-house of success."

The "round-house of success"—that is the goal of all of us! It is your *goal!*

The six volumes that go to make up EFFECTIVE SPEECH were written especially to help you in attaining success in your chosen field of endeavor.

Every man and woman, young or old, who is interested in greater *achievement,* must face the fact that no one is independent, that one's business or social success is dependent upon the ability to impress upon others one's personality, and the value to *them* of what one has to offer. This applies equally to the young man seeking a worth-while position and to the corporation president asking his Board of Directors for a vote of confidence.

Everything we get out of life depends upon our ability to influence others.

We do this in two ways—by our actions, and by our speech.

The man who can "get his ideas across," either by individual conversation or by addressing a group, has a tremendous advantage.

Speech is the very foundation of all business relations. It is the most direct way of influencing others. If a business is to be efficiently and effectively conducted, it must be "shot through" with EFFECTIVE SPEECH.

Executives must instruct and direct their subordinates. They must call together department heads and talk over general policies. The department heads, in turn, must call together their subordinates to explain these policies in detail, and to consult with them in regard to the best methods of executing them.

Subordinates must seek out their chiefs and suggest improvements in manufacture, advertising methods, sales policies, office procedure, salary adjustments, display of merchandise, management of personnel, and many other matters.

Sales, the adjustment of complaints, the origination of new enterprises, all these depend for their success upon EFFECTIVE SPEECH.

No luke-warm, stereotyped, emasculated expression of an idea—no matter how good the idea may be—will ever accomplish much. Ideas must be *sharpened to a point* by *vivid statement*, expressed in *living words*, if they are to be driven home to others.

Big business always "bids up" the man who has given thought to his speech habits. The "talking Vice-President" is a permanent institution. *The day has arrived when the ability to talk fluently and convincingly must be regarded as the* IRREDUCIBLE MINIMUM OF PREPARATION *for business.*

Most businesses today realize that their officers, and even all their executives, must be prepared to accept speaking invitations from Rotary Clubs, Advertising Clubs, and many other organizations. *Such speakers become ambassadors of goodwill,* creators of the MOST VALUABLE PUBLICITY IN THE WORLD!

Speech, effectively employed, will ensure you a hearing from the most indifferent. It will bring a sense of joy and achievement to your work. It will heighten your efficiency. It will transform you from the man you are into the man you wish to be.

If you aspire to rise above the crowd, to reach the goal of *leadership,* you *must* SPEAK EFFECTIVELY!

Words are tools—the most amazing and important yet invented by the human brain. They possess the lightness of the wind, yet the power of thunderbolts.

The mind can gather facts; reason can draw conclusions; imagination clothe them in rainbow colors; *but it is the spoken word that lights them with the blazing fires of conviction.*

The Master understood this. He chose to *speak* his message. He left not one written line, for he knew speaking is nature's own method of instruction.

Century after century, the history of nations can be followed through the lives of men whose *speech* has shaped the course of events.

The day of flowery oratory has passed. What is demanded today is straight-from-the-shoulder, hard-hitting, convincing talk. Self-confidence, command of the right word in the right place, and ability to think on one's feet are indispensable.

Now, to help you in all this is the purpose of these volumes in Effective Speech. They contain the fundamentals of speaking, either in private conference or on the public platform, and the instruction is not confused or obscured by theory and long-winded dissertation. It is definite, business-like instruction. One of the most forceful speakers America has ever had once said that real eloquence is the speech of "a man who says what he means and means what he says." In that respect, EFFECTIVE SPEECH may be said to teach eloquence, for it shows a man who has something to say how to get down to brass tacks and *say it!*

The keynote of EFFECTIVE SPEECH is *how to go straight to the point.* It deals with clear and convincing speech; with the expression of ideas in forms that will impress the hearer. The simplicity of methods and conciseness of language which it emphasizes will make a particularly strong appeal to the person who *wants results*—AND WANTS THEM QUICKLY!

A brief perusal of the Table of Contents of Effective Speech will reveal to you, whether you are an experienced speaker or are just beginning to study, the most vital needs in the speaking of today, and will direct you in the way of developing your style in all of them or in the few in which you find yourself weak.

Consider then the advantages that EFFECTIVE SPEECH will bring you. Look ahead and find ways by which you can improve your speech habits. And, if you persist, if you keep working, if you practice, if you master what is here presented, you will find yourself "looking ahead," down the main-line track, to the "round-house of success!"

—DWIGHT E. WATKINS.

Effective Speech

MANUAL I

GETTING READY TO SPEAK

TABLE OF CONTENTS

MANUAL I

MANUAL I

GETTING READY TO SPEAK

PART A

PERSONAL DEVELOPMENT

"The Chairman will now call upon Mr. Harrison for a few remarks in connection with this notable occasion—the twentieth anniversary of the founding of this business,—Mr. Harrison, our beloved 'Jim,' a man who has been with us from that very first day when we opened offices down in the old building on James Street. Jim Harrison!" (Applause!)

Mr. Harrison arose, tipped over his chair, tried to pick it up, failed to get it up quickly, and was finally helped in righting it by friends at his side. He was red in the face, was trembling, and was much embarrassed. When he finally got the chair right side up, he wiped his perspiring brow with his napkin and then put the napkin in his pocket.

Then he began:

"Er—I—er—(then he cleared his throat) —ahem—I—er—(whispering to Smith at his right) What shall I say? (Then to the chairman), Bill, I mean Mr. Jones—I mean, Mr. Presiding Officer—I—er—I—ahem—tonight—I—uh—tonight—is—Really, Bill, I don't know anything to say—What did you call on me anyway for—you know I can't make any speech! (The Chairman: Tell 'em something about your long experience with us!) Yes—I—er—I—uh—might."

Here he reached for his glass of water and upset it. His friend Smith picked it up and poured a little water out of the water-bottle into it. Then Mr. Harrison took a swallow, and set the glass down squarely on his spoon! And it promptly upset again! Everybody was now roaring with laughter and "Jim" was getting redder and redder. He hunted for his napkin to wipe his brow and finally picked up Smith's. He wiped his forehead with it, and then put *it* in his pocket. This was too much! The crowd *roared* with laughter, and cries of "Give him yours, Jones," etc., rang about the tables. Finally Harrison fairly yelled:

"Oh, go on with your d——d banquet and leave me out of it," and sat down, feeling that he never could show his face in the office again!

Then the Chairman said:

"I'm sure we all know Jim *can* make a good speech. He just didn't get off right, that's all. Hereafter we're going to have the chairs all nailed to the floor and the water glasses fitted with running-shoe spikes, so we can make 'em stick where we want them to. We know Jim is the best talker in our organization and that he could sell palm-leaf fans to the Esquimaux! Give him a hand, Gentlemen!"

And there was a rousing round of applause, but it didn't make "Jim" feel much better.

Then the Chairman said again:

"Perhaps we may now hear from one who, although he has not been with us as long as Jim Harrison, has nevertheless made an enviable record—Mr. Charles Blake, in charge of our Northern Territory. Mr. Blake!" (Applause.)

Mr. Blake arose, deftly slipped his chair back, smiled, nodded slightly in response to the applause, and began:

"Mr. Toastmaster, and fellow workers in the James-Walrath Company:

"Theodore Roosevelt once told a story about a man who . . ." Then he told a good story—one that made everybody feel that Jim Harrison was, after all, one of the mainstays of the company, and a story that made everybody like Charles Blake, too. Then he told in an interesting way of his association with the company: how he had encountered many amusing incidents along the way; how at times he had been in the depths of despair, but how the sky had always brightened; how there had been many changes in the policy of the company—each one of a forward-looking nature, preparing the way for greater accomplishment; and how there had always been a wonderful spirit of co-operation and fellowship abroad within the organization; and how, finally, he believed that now the company was about to take a great step forward—one that was particularly fitting for the coming year, the year during which the company was to attain its majority and take its stand among the great companies of the country.

When he sat down he was greeted with tremendous applause, and the nods of approval were such that everyone was certain that Charles Blake was going to be one of the great men of the company in the years that were to follow.

NOW!

You wish to avoid such a failure as Mr. Harrison made.

You wish to succeed as Mr. Blake did.

VERY WELL!

This course was created for exactly that purpose.

But, first, before you begin your real study of this course, I wish to have a heart-to-heart talk with you.

I wish to tell you what a *wise decision* you made when you enrolled for this training.

ABILITY TO SPEAK CLEARLY AND FORCEFULLY, WHETHER IN BUSINESS OR IN SOCIAL LIFE, WILL DO MORE TO HELP YOU GAIN SUCCESS THAN ANYTHING ELSE IN THE WORLD.

I will show you why.

LISTEN:

Whether you succeed in life or not depends not so much on *what you do* as on *what sort of a person you are*, and this course on *"Effective Speech"* will *make you a better person!*

FIRST, it will help you *think more clearly.* Many men really do not know what they think. Their minds are full of half-developed opinions. This course will do away with your half-developed opinions, because speaking *makes you say your thoughts in words*, and *no half-formed thought can be expressed in words.* Further, many men are inconsistent in their thinking. When *one certain thought* is present in their minds they believe *one way*, and when *some other thought* is present they believe *another way*. Speaking will compel you to consider all thoughts on a given subject at one time—or within a very short limit of time—and will further compel you to give attention to their *relative worth*, and to arrive at a *correct decision* as to *which is best*. This will clear up your thinking. As a result of clear thinking, you will learn to *reason more successfully*. You will be able to hold your thoughts in mind, and, step by step, *perceive their relations*, thus arriving at a more *dependable conclusion*. By all this, too, you will be able to *get other people to listen to you*, for they will be able to follow your thought.

SECOND, this course will enable you to state your ideas *expertly*. Words, sentences, and paragraphs are the means of stating ideas, and such constant use as you will make of them in this course will give you the ability to state your ideas with *ease* and *accuracy*. You will learn the *meanings of words*. You will learn *correct grammatical forms*. You will become *skilful in the construction of your sentences*. You will *group your sentences well*, forming good paragraphs. In short, you will gain the power of *using words* to *make your fellowmen do what you want them to do.*

THIRD, this course, if you put into practice the things you learn, will *strengthen your emotions.* It will enable you to reveal *how you feel about what you say.* You will no longer stifle your feelings. Your *face will become more expressive.* Your *eyes will become more responsive.* You will *approve more enthusiastically,* and *denounce more energetically.* Intellect may be the throttle of the human machine, the place where control is applied, but emotion is the boiler, the source of all power. In this course you will learn to be *a more forceful personality.*

NOW REVIEW!

Go back over the three benefits I have already said you will receive from this course. Can you look away from the book and give them? Try it! If you cannot give them easily, take another look at them and try it again.

Can you think of any subject that has come up in your conversation of the last few days upon which your opinions were rather "hazy"? Stop, and try to find one. What was it? Have you any definite opinions on it now? If you have, can you give one or two reasons why you hold your opinion?

Can you think of any time during the last few days when you failed to state some idea expertly? What was it? Can you state it better now?

Do you remember any one of your acquaintances who, within the last few days, has expressed some idea with a good deal of feeling? Do you think you could express it as forcefully? Could you express it *more* forcefully?

Repeat again the three benefits I have thus far promised you will gain from this course.

NOW LISTEN AGAIN!

Here are *two more benefits* that you will secure from this course.

FIRST, you are going to *improve your appearance.* I do not mean you are going to improve your manner of dressing—although you probably will do that. I mean you are going to improve your *general carriage. Your shoulders will become straighter. Your chest will be held higher. Your legs will be more alertly and firmly placed.* Your *movements will become more sure and more graceful.* Carlyle once said, "A hero is known by his gait." If you will do what I tell you in this course, your *whole body will become instinct with thought and emotion.*

You will develop dignity, poise and power.

SECOND, you are going to *improve your voice* by the study of this course. Your voice will become *louder without becoming unpleasant.* Your voice will become richer. Your voice will be less monotonous, that is, will have *greater variety and attractiveness.* These characteristics will be seen in your *social chat* as well as in your more *formal speaking.*

NOW REVIEW AGAIN.

Can you state, without looking at the book, the last two benefits that I have mentioned? Try it.

When you have given the first benefit, namely, that your appearance will be improved, can you state some of the *ways* in which it will be improved?

When you have given the second benefit, namely, that your voice will be improved, can you state some of the *ways* in which it will be improved?

CAN YOU CONCENTRATE?

The word concentrate is rather a big word, but it stands for a very simple thing. To concentrate upon a thing means to bring to bear upon that thing your *whole mental power,* to *see it thoroughly,* to *observe its details.*

Do you remember the picture of the big bull that is used to advertise "Bull Durham" smoking tobacco? Did you ever notice that the *white spot* on the bull's back is really a *map of the United States?* If you have not noticed that fact, then you have failed to concentrate upon that picture of the bull!

Well, this course will teach you how to concentrate. It will teach you that when you observe a thing, you must *observe it closely.* When you wish to describe a pleasure trip after you have studied this course, you will not only tell what you *saw* but what you *heard,* what *pleasant odors* you perceived, what *good food* you ate, and whether the *air* was *moist* or *dry, warm* or *cool, hot* or *cold.* You will in other words be able to describe your trip more fully, because you concentrated, *observed closely* all its features.

You will learn to concentrate not only upon *things* but also upon *ideas.* When the word *industries* is used, for example, you will see *factories, workers, machines,* etc. You will think of the *steel industry,* the *lumber industry,* etc. Perhaps you will have sought out the meanings of the word that the dictionary gives. Suppose you do that now! Or if you are utilizing your spare moments in reading this little book on a street car, or train, or ferryboat, jot the word down on a slip of paper out of your notebook and "look up" the word in the dictionary when you get home.

NOTICE THIS!

Are you aware that in this short paragraph I have given you *three ways* of preparing yourself to speak well?

FIRST, you should *utilize your spare moments* in improving your *store of ideas* and *methods of thinking*. There is no need to read the entire newspaper, giving attention to every petty item, and usually forgetting most of what is read by the time the paper is laid down. It is better to read the *headlines* and a *few selected articles*, and then give your time to *more solid reading*. Most men who are effective speakers are very jealous of their time, and use *every moment of it* in doing something that will prepare them for something bigger and better that they wish to do. If you will cultivate the habit of reading something worth while during the time that you usually *waste*, you will be doing *one* thing that will help you become a good speaker.

SECOND, I have asked you to carry a pocket notebook in which you may jot down thoughts that come to you, topics to be investigated, or words whose meaning or pronunciation you desire to find out from the dictionary. Nearly all good speakers have the "notebook habit."

THIRD, I have asked you to consult a dictionary. Anyone who desires to speak well should have a good dictionary. Get a copy of Webster's Collegiate Dictionary (be sure it is published by G. & C. Merriam Co., Springfield, Mass.) or a desk-size copy of The Standard Dictionary (published by Funk & Wagnalls Co., New York). These desk-size dictionaries are sufficient for all ordinary purposes, and are less expensive than the larger ones.

These three things that I have just brought to your attention, if acted upon, would, *in themselves,* within a year *make you a much better speaker.* Many a business man today would give *hundreds of dollars* to have cultivated these habits during the last ten years. BUT NOW TO RETURN!

A moment ago I said this course would help you *concentrate upon ideas.* It will also help you to concentrate upon *arguments.* It will help you see *just what a speaker or writer is trying to prove.* It will help you see *just how he is proving it.* You will be able to see whether he is *relying upon facts* or is *quoting opinions.* You will notice whether he is *assuming too much.* You can detect *whether his conclusion necessarily* follows from the information he has presented. You can expose any tendency to *ignore the real point* of the argument. You will be able to see whether *any example* that he quotes is *applicable to the present case.*

Yes, this course will enable you to *concentrate,* and any successful man, in any walk of life, will tell you that when you have learned to concentrate you *have the battle half won!*

BUT AGAIN!

This course will *widen and deepen your interests.* You will learn to read more intently than you have ever read before, for you will be *seeking eagerly* for something that you can *make use of in your speaking.* You will wish to store in your memory a part of the information you glean from your reading. To do this you will go back over what you have read and strive to impress it upon your mind. Such a process *deepens* your interest. Very likely you will often find in your reading a reference to something that you do not fully understand. If you cultivate the habit of following up such matters, you will soon be reading articles in the encyclopedias, and may even be buying books on certain matters. You will *widen your interests* until soon *the whole range of our modern complex living will become of interest* to you. *Many business men and women have dated a period of widened vision* and *increased profits* from the day on which they began a study of *effective speaking.*

LOOK AT THIS LIST.

Here is what this course will do for you. It will help you:

1. Think more clearly.
2. State your ideas more expertly.
3. Strengthen your emotions.
4. Improve your appearance.
5. Improve your voice.
6. Concentrate.
7. Widen and deepen your interests.

NOW LET ME PROVE IT!

When you began reading this first lesson, you had a rather hazy idea that a study of speaking would benefit you. Your idea *was* hazy, wasn't it? Now you know *seven distinct benefits* that a study of speaking will bring you. Have I not already set you on the road to *think more clearly?*

Early in this lesson I asked you to rest a moment and state the three benefits of this course that I had already mentioned. If you did as I told you, you *stated your ideas more expertly* than you could have done before you read this lesson.

I have been talking to you now, through these pages, for five or six minutes. You already had a *vague feeling* that this course might benefit you, but do you not now feel *much more strongly* that it will be of value to you to pursue this course? In fact, has there not risen up inside of you a *great determination* that speaking is *worth while*, and that *you can do what others have done?*

Have you not already, too, determined that you will stand up straighter, hold your chest higher, and *enter into life more fully?* Have you not already straightened up in your seat? Have I not already *improved your appearance?*

I haven't given you as yet, I admit, any exercise to strengthen your voice, but I dare say that if you were to say to a friend *"You ought to learn to speak,"* you would say it with a *ring in your voice* that would *carry conviction.* You have already improved your voice by having *deepened your belief in the truth.*

Did it take some effort a moment ago to recall the three first benefits of this course? Did you find that in reality you had not been concentrating on what you read? And did you not *then, right at that moment,* get your first lesson in concentrating?

This is only *Part A* of the *First Lesson* and I have only given you about *one third* of what I shall give *just on getting ready to speak!* But if you have done what I told you to do as we went along, *you have entered a new world. You have left your old world behind you. You have faced a new and better future.*

Part B

PERSONAL ADVANCEMENT

In *Part A* of this lesson I told you how this course would *make you a better man.*

Now I am going to tell you how it will *bring you advancement.*

This course will bring you advancement because it will help you "sell yourself." (By "selling yourself" I mean bringing yourself favorably to the attention of others, so that they will *like* you, *employ* you, *promote* you, or *do what you want them to do.*) It will help you "sell yourself" without making you *crude* or *offensive.* You will *not* become *egotistic.* The publicity that effective speaking gives a man is *the very best publicity,* for, like the best sort of advertising, it is *indirect.*

Consider a typical case:

Mr. A. is one day invited to speak at a banquet given by his firm to its employees. He is invited *not* because those in charge of the banquet know he can make a good speech, but because one of their speakers has failed them at the last moment and they know that Mr. A. has been studying a course in effective speaking. They feel it will be somewhat of a joke to put him on the program, and he can't very well spoil the whole evening, for the other speakers can well save the day. So they put him on the program. But, contrary to their expectations, Mr. A. makes an excellent speech, in fact, one of the hits of the evening. He is quite unknown, and when he sits down people about the tables ask one another who he is and what his position is. Thus his name is passed perhaps a hundred times among the banqueters. On the way home, the guests remark about his speech and he is mentioned as "a bright fellow." Some of the executives have heard him. They talk him over. The next week one of the vice-presidents has a particularly hard task to perform in the way of announcing a new firm policy to the employees, and he casts about for someone to help him. At once he thinks of Mr. A., who spoke at the banquet. Mr. A. is called in and given a place on a committee to talk the matter over. In the committee meeting he presents his ideas clearly, logically, forcefully. His suggestions are seen to be wise, and they are adopted by the committee, and later they work out successfully in launching the new policy. As a result Mr. A. is put in permanent charge of relationships with employees, at an increase in salary. Other firms in the city have men in similar positions. He meets them—men whom he could not have met before he made the speech at the banquet. They talk over their problems. Again he has good ideas to offer, and presents them in good form. In a year or so he is elected president of the Personnel Managers Association, and this results in his being called by a larger firm to take charge of their personnel work.

So it went. And it was all done *without any crude pushing,* through *ability to speak.*

Perhaps other men had just as good ideas as Mr. A., but he secured his first opportunity to *advertise himself* through *speaking*, and he continued to advance his interests by his *ability to think and to express himself well!*

Now banquets are not the only places where this course will aid you in advancing your interests.

This course will help you in *Business Conferences*. If you are *really alive*, you will be called upon at *some* time—perhaps *often*—to present your ideas before your associates, and if at such times you can present your ideas *clearly* (with *sound facts* and *striking examples*), logically (arranging your ideas in a *convincing order*), and *forcefully* (with *good physical vigor, good voice*, and *pleasing bearing*), you will be sure to draw favorable attention to yourself, such attention, indeed, as may well *bring you promotion*. It is in business conferences that men "size up" one another, and by studying this course, you can *make yourself a leader*, one *not afraid* to *take the controlling hand*, one *whom others will gladly follow*.

This course will help you in *Sales-Talks*. It will help you *analyze* your proposition. It will enable you to *seize upon the important ar-*

guments for buying your particular product. It will help you *arrange these arguments in the most effective order.* It will help you *choose the best words* to present your arguments. There is always *one best way* to present any proposition and this course will help you discover *that way.* And *if* you can improve your *selling ability,* it will follow as surely as day follows night, and *you know it*—that *you will secure advancement.*

This course will help you in *Writing Letters.* The Secretary of a Young Men's Christian Association in an Ohio city based a membership campaign letter upon a *single* lesson and was pleased to find that *that letter brought more replies per hundred copies than any letter ever sent out from his office.* This course will help you write letters of equal *compelling power.* And if you can write letters that will *accomplish what you wish them to accomplish—again, you know it*—you can secure *more business,* and *more business always, without fail,* will bring you *more money,* either in *profits,* if you are in business for yourself, or *increased salary,* if you are in the employ of someone else.

This course will help you in *Preparing Advertisements.* It will give you the fundamentals of *psychology,* and *psychology is the science upon which advertising is based.* If you study this course thoroughly, you will *lay hold* of the *motives that move men to action,* and you will unconsciously use these in preparing your advertising "copy"—and once more you *know* that *to be able to write a better "ad"* than the "other fellow" means that you will be given preference.

This course will help you *Educate the Public.* "Educate the Public" is a great slogan with many public utility corporations and other large combinations of capital. So much is this phase of corporation management emphasized that there are now literally hundreds of *"talking vice-presidents"* in the country. Usually these men are *men taken from the ranks,* but always *men who have attracted attention as speakers.* Constantly such positions are being created and many opportunities are opening up to those who have been alert enough to prepare for them. Perhaps a position as a "talking vice-president" will be offered *you,* if you profit by this course.

This course will help you *Aid the Community. The largest service a speaker can render is the service he can render his community,* and this often *brings very sudden elevation to positions of trust and promi-*

nence. If a man can successfully address a large gathering such as a Rotary Club, a Kiwanis Club, or a citizens' mass meeting, he becomes *very widely known* and his *name carries influence. Such men are valuable assets* to any firm or corporation, and they are *constantly being offered positions.* You will be neglecting one of your *surest avenues of advancement,* if you fail to become a speaker who can *speak well on civic problems* before your local clubs and civic organizations.

This course, last of all, will help you in *Politics.* Every man who aspires to public office must be able to *tell the people what he proposes to do if elected.* He must speak to *various small clubs.* He must address *mass meetings.* He must *issue statements.* He must *convince individual voters* of his knowledge and ability. This course will *help you do these things well.* Often a political position brings *additional remuneration.* Often it so advertises a man that he secures *more business.* If you can *talk well to individuals,* if you can *carry on a successful political campaign,* you will open up a *new source of personal power in your community.*

NOW REVIEW!

Can you state the *one big benefit* that this

course will bring you in securing personal advancement?

Can you relate the case of Mr. A. without looking at the book? Try it.

Can you enumerate the *seven ways* in which you may secure power through this course? Try it.

If you have difficulty in remembering all *seven,* suppose you try to remember just the first *five.* Do you notice that these *five* deal with business in some way? And do you notice that the last *two* deal with community activities? Now, try to remember the *first five,* and then the *last two.*

Here is the way a speaker's outline would look if he were to make a speech on *Ways of Securing Advancement through Effective Speech.*

Effective Speech will help a man:

A. In Business
1. In Business Conferences
2. In Sales Talks
3. In Writing Letters
4. In Preparing Advertisements
5. In Educating the Public

B. In Community Life
1. In Discussing Community Problems
2. In Politics

Notice carefully the grouping of the headings in the outline just given. It is always helpful to arrange headings in this way. It aids *you in thinking more logically* and it helps you in *remembering what you have to say.*

NOW, MAKE YOUR FIRST SPEECH

If you are at home alone, read over this *Part B* of this lesson, and then stand up and, without looking at the book, talk for a little while on this matter of securing advancement through speaking. If you still have difficulty in remembering the headings, copy on a card, in large handwriting, the outline that has just been given you, and stand up by your chair and give a short talk. *Imagine clearly your audience* and *just talk to them. Do not imagine you are making a speech* but just give them some *strong, fatherly advice!*

If you happen to be reading this lesson at some place where you cannot give this little talk at once, *do it as soon as you get alone at home.*

NOW, DON'T PUT OFF THIS LITTLE TALK

The only way to learn to swim is to *go into the water,* and the only way to learn to speak, is to *make a speech!*

Part C

OVERCOMING FEAR IN SPEAKING

The *assistant cashier* of a bank once said to me: "I'm all right when I have to talk to *just one man across my desk,* but whenever I have to *stand on my feet* and speak even to *just a dozen men I'm scared to death!"*

Yet that man today is *president of a great National Bank,* is chairman of almost all the local "drive" committees, and makes hundreds of speeches a year before the largest and most educated audiences of the community.

He conquered *his* fear in speaking.

You can conquer *yours.*

I know you *tremble.* I know your *knees shake.* I know you *can't keep your notes from quivering in your hand.* I know that you are *short of breath,* that your *heart beats a tattoo against your ribs,* that *your temples throb,* that you *get red in the face,* that *cold shivers run up and down your spine,* that you *stammer* and *stutter,* that your *mouth gets dry,* and that you have a *"terrible in-*

ward churning" in the general region of your stomach.

BUT LISTEN!

I have seen *hundreds* of cases of this fear of speaking, *but I never yet saw a student of speaking who did not get over this fear if he persisted! Here are a few simple rules to overcome this fear.*

FIRST: KNOW MORE ABOUT YOUR SUBJECT THAN ANYBODY IN YOUR AUDIENCE. Then you won't fear them on the score of subject matter, at least. You will be master of the situation.

SECOND: MAKE YOURSELF MASTER OF THE WORDS YOU USE. If you are sure you can *pronounce correctly* all the words you use, if you are *sure of their meanings,* you will remove your fear as far as your vocabulary is concerned.

THIRD: BE SURE YOU USE CORRECT GRAMMAR. Do not let any sentence get away from your lips that you know is not properly constructed. *One of the later lessons in this course* will help you in your use of words and proper grammatical constructions. If you give careful attention to this matter for a short while, you will find your fear greatly decreasing.

FOURTH: GIVE ATTENTION TO YOUR APPEARANCE. Dress neatly, and properly for the occasion. Be sure you stand in a good position (one of the later lessons deals with this matter), learn how to make your gestures correctly. When you have mastered these little matters of appearance you will feel much more at home.

FIFTH: GO SLOWLY AND BREATHE DEEPLY. This is perhaps the *most important direction of all.* When you rise and address the chairman, take time to look over your audience, and make several pauses during a single sentence. Be sure you get a good breath after each part of your sentence, and, if necessary to secure composure, take *two* or *three* breaths at the ends of your sentences. At the start of your speech just "*fire minute guns.*" You can go more rapidly later.

Now, you would probably say to me, if you *could,* that all of this is *going to take some time. Of course it will!* But I ask you *is anything in this life that is worth while easy?* You are undertaking this course so that *you can advance more rapidly than the other fellow.* In this course is the information that you need to enable you to accomplish the task you have set out to do. *Make use of it! Persist in your undertaking.* And just as you persist, just as you devote time and energy to your problem, you will surpass your associates who are not willing to do what you are doing. Really, *you ought to thank a kind Providence* who made so many people with the inability to stick to a task until it is accomplished. By *their very failures, you* will be enabled to rise above them.

Speak before your fellows every time you can get an opportunity. By and by you will *get used to it.* Then you will have no fear.

JUST TWO WORDS MORE

Have you self-control?

Can you stick to a task although it *is* uncomfortable?

Then let me tell you something.

This fear is much more apparent to *you* than to *those to whom you speak!* Often men have told me they were "frightened to death" while they were speaking, and yet to *us who were in the audience* they appeared to be *perfectly at ease.* They gave this appearance *because they had self-control. You can do the same.* (In a later lesson I shall tell you how to *handle your notes* so that they will not be seen to tremble.) If you will only "keep your head" and *assume an outward calm,* you can still be badly frightened and yet *not let it be known to your audience at all!*

Again, *your fear will subside after the first few sentences*—as soon as you *forget yourself* and *become interested in your topic.*

Abraham Lincoln is a superb illustration of how interest in one's topic will free one from embarrassment. His biographer, William Herndon, says of him: "At first he was very awkward and it seemed a real labor to adjust himself to his surroundings. He struggled for a time under a feeling of apparent diffidence and sensitiveness. . . . As he moved along in his speech he became freer and less uneasy in his movements." Joseph H. Choate gives similar testimony in regard to him. Says he: "At first sight, there was nothing impressing and imposing about him. His clothes hung awkwardly on his giant frame. His seamed and rugged features bore the furrows of hardship and struggle. As he talked to me before the meeting, he seemed ill at ease, with that sort of apprehension which a young man might feel before presenting himself to a new and strange audience, whose critical disposition he dreaded. . . . When he spoke, he was transformed; his eye kindled, his voice rang, his face shone and seemed to light up the whole assembly."

So *you* can succeed, even though you are slightly embarrassed, and you may make a *great speech* after the first few moments *by becoming interested in your topic.*

Part D

METHODS OF PREPARING AND DELIVERING A SPEECH

Four different methods of preparing and delivering a speech are given by the authorities on public speaking.

I. Writing Out the Speech and Reading It

LANGUAGE TOO HIGHLY POLISHED

This method of preparing and delivering a speech is perhaps the worst. It is bad, in the first place, because we do not write as we speak. Writing gives time for careful *selection of words,* for *working out sentences that are long* and *involved,* for *studied effects,* and, in general, for what is known as "*polish.*" All of this, as a rule, *deprives* the speech of *directness* and *vitality.* After a speech is written, the writer goes over it carefully, and noticing some *common word,* thinks that perhaps a better word could be substituted. At once he goes to his dictionary, or book of synonyms, and gets a *bigger* and more *high-sounding word* and substitutes it for the more common one. Not *once* does he do this, but *many times* in the course of his speech. He notices, too, a number of *short sentences,* perhaps, and he *combines them into one longer sentence.* He carefully *works out his imagery,* developing it to its highest extent. He *works out long and intricate contrasts.* He *builds climaxes* which abound in the *flowers* and *ornaments of rhetoric.* All of this he does until the written speech is far removed in its style from the manner of direct conversation. As a result, the audience notices the difference, *finds greater difficulty in understanding the speech,* and, fatigued by the difficulty, *grows restless* and *inattentive.* The speech *loses the effect of sincerity.* The speaker, the audience feels, is giving them *not* what he *thinks* and *feels* about the *subject at the moment,* but what he thought and felt about it *a week or ten days before.* The speech *"smells of the lamp,"* as the saying goes, and much of its *power is lost.*

LOSS OF THE POWER OF THE EYE

A second disadvantage of writing and reading lies in the fact that the speaker *loses the power of the eye.* The eye is the most important of the agents of expression. By it are many of the most subtle and telling effects secured by a speaker. The eye becomes bright with the sparkle of humor, or is dimmed by sorrow. The brow wrinkles in concentration or anger. The lids of the eye narrow or open wide as the mood of the speaker changes. All of these changes are lost to the audience, when a speaker must confine his eye to a manuscript. Further, the speaker cannot discipline and control his audience when reading. Every audience has restless, inattentive, or hostile members in it. *Often a glance or a steady gaze will bring these people back to attention.* A speaker can detect restless portions in his audience and can overcome the restlessness before it spreads to other portions. But the speaker who reads has no time for these things, as he must be busy reading the words of his manuscript.

Vocal Flexibility Hampered

But one of the greatest disadvantages of reading is that *the voice in reading follows an entirely different path from what it does in conversation or direct speaking.* In conversation the path of the voice is characterized by great variety and sudden changes. In reading the voice follows a fairly level path without many marked changes. Proof of this is found in the fact that if one were listening outside a school-room door, he could at once tell whether the pupils within were *reading* to their teacher or *talking* to her. It is true, an expert reader may, to some extent, overcome this fault in reading, but it is only now and then that one discovers a reader expert enough to entirely disguise his reading. The best of readers have difficulty in divesting themselves of the monotonous pitch and the regular time that usually go with gleaning and conveying thought from the printed page.

Vocal Apparatus Cramped and Misdirected

Then, also, the vocal apparatus is usually cramped and misdirected in reading. No yell leader before the bleachers at any of the great football games would direct his megaphone at the ground. Rather he directs it into the bleachers where the people are. Yet nearly always the person who reads his speeches, directs his voice toward his manuscript, the desk, and the floor, rather than out toward the audience. Further, by the position of the head, the muscles of the throat and upper chest are constricted. The sound of the voice does not have a free path to the outside air, and resonance and carrying power are reduced.

Reading Sometimes the Best Method

In spite of all these disadvantages, however, there are times when the reading of a carefully prepared address seems fitting. Presidents of the United States, Senators, Members of Congress, and prominent political leaders often write out and read their speeches to avoid being misquoted. Generally the occasions on which such men speak are occasions of importance, and great care must be exercised in determining what is said. By writing and reading, any ill-advised wordings or sudden bursts of feeling that might be disastrous, are avoided. If there is garbling or misrepresentation of the speech by newspapers or periodicals there can be definite reference to exactly what was said. On certain occasions, too—occasions of somewhat formal or ceremonial character, such as Washington's Birthday, Memorial Day, or the anniversary of the founding of some institution, a carefully prepared address read from manuscript may seem in order. On such occasions the speaker is often invited long beforehand, and is supposed to have devoted much time and thought to what he has to say. A manuscript lives up to this presumption, and seems to add worth and dignity. Further, these addresses are often afterwards printed, and it is well to have them in such exact and definite form as will bring out their literary merit. Technical addresses also, because careful statement is needed, and because figures and statistics are often employed, may well be read from manuscript.

II. Writing Out the Speech and Committing it to Memory

Faults largely the Same as Those Found in Reading

This method has many of the *same faults* as are found in the method of *writing* and *reading*. The language used is stilted and artificial just as it is in the manuscript style. The sentence structure is involved and the effects studied. The path of the voice, too, is very likely to be level and to lack variety just as is the case in reading, for, after all, the speaker is really reading, only in speaking from memory he is reading from a mental page instead of from a page that is seen by the audience. True, an expert elocutionist may be able somewhat to deceive his audience, but such speakers are rare.

No Chance for Adaptations to Audience

Again, no chance is given in a committed speech for adaptation to unforeseen circumstances in the occasion or audience. The speech must be delivered as it was committed to memory, for, if changes are made, the association of ideas by which the various sentences are remembered is destroyed, and it is well nigh impossible to pick up the thread of the discourse again.

Little Re-creation of Thought

Further, the whole personality of the speaker does not react at the time of speaking. The mind is engaged in remembering words and sentence forms and cannot devote adequate attention to re-creating the thought at the time of utterance.

Gestures Likely to be Ineffective

Gestures are likely to be ill-timed, to be just a fraction of a second too early or too late. The gestures, also, being generally developed for their own sakes, being practiced as something apart from the thought, are not likely to be very successful in revealing the true feeling of the moment, if indeed there be real feeling in the committed speech. The body does not reinforce the gestures of the hands and arms, either. Sometimes the gestures are good and the speaking is good, but the two do not synchronize, do not seem to be parts of an organic whole.

Speech May be Forgotten

But the greatest objection to writing out a speech and memorizing it is that it is likely to be forgotten. The memory is one of the most unreliable functions of the mind, and scarcely is there a speaker who uses the *memoriter* style who has not gone through the excruciating experience of forgetting. If a single word in a sentence happens to be changed, the verbal associations are broken up and often it is impossible to go on. When a speaker has once forgotten a speech, also, he is never quite so much at home before an audience again. Always in the back of his head is the fear that a similar experience may overtake him again. Consequently he cannot do his best work because part of his attention is on his speech and part of it on forgetting.

Involves Great Labor

Another objection that applies to writing and committing a speech is that it involves a tremendous amount of labor. It is no small task just to push the pen through the words of a speech of thirty minutes or an hour, and when the additional work of committing these words is imposed, the task is indeed staggering. Many men who have pursued this style through many years have been forced to abandon it in middle life simply because their constitutions could not stand such gruelling labor.

OF USE, HOWEVER, IN TRAINING A SPEAKER

It may be said, however, of writing and committing that it is of use in the training of a speaker. A little writing of speeches is likely to call the attention of the student to carelessness in his use of English, and to open his eyes to some of the finer points of style. Likewise, when a speech is committed to memory, and its delivery drilled upon, much improvement in the use of the voice and gestures can be secured. But the drill should not be indulged in until the speaker can do well in no other style. The *memoriter* style should quickly be abandoned before it gets too strong a hold, and should be used only as a drill for useful exercise.

III. The Extemporaneous Method

The third method of preparing and delivering a speech is known as the *extempore* (look up this word in your dictionary) or extemporaneous method, by which is meant that the outline, or path of the thought, is carefully prepared so that the speaker knows beforehand just what thoughts he will utter, but that he leaves the exact language in which these thoughts will be clothed until his appearance before the audience.

The Extemporaneous Style not to be Confused with the Impromptu Style

This *extempore* style should be carefully distinguished from the *impromptu* style, by which is meant that the speaker prepares neither thought nor words before the actual speaking. Let it be said in regard to the *impromptu* style that very little good speaking results from it. *Impromptu* speeches are likely to be loosely built and to be built of slight material. It is true that now and again every speaker will be forced to speak *impromptu,* but such occasions are rare, and when good speaking results it will be found either that the speaker falls back upon other previous speeches he has made upon the same topic, or that the subject matter of his speech is thoroughly known by him and has become a part of his daily routine, so that his outline is ready-made to his hand. In the extemporaneous method the thoughts are never left to the moment. The speaker knows exactly his goal and the means he will employ to reach it.

Notes Optional

Whether notes should be carried before the audience or not depends upon the individual and the complexity of the outline. If the speaker finds it easy to carry an outline in his mind, he should by all means do it, and not depend on notes before an audience. On the other hand if the speaker has difficulty in remembering an outline, there is nothing wrong in carrying notes upon the platform.

Notes Should be Properly Prepared and Properly Used

Let it be said, however, that no attempt should be made to conceal these notes. They should not be hidden in the palm of the hand, nor behind the speaker. Often the speaker can make gestures with the hand in which the notes are held. The notes should be written on only one side of cards about the size of a postal card or a library filing card (3x5), and the writing should be large enough to allow the speaker to catch the words from the waist-line, so that there will be no need to lift the card closely before the eyes in order to catch the next heading. Notes should never be written on both sides of a card, for the card will be sure to be wrong-side-up when the notes are needed. The card should never be folded, for often the card is found to be folded up when the notes are needed, and a pause in the speech is necessary while the speaker unfolds the card and finds the desired place.

Neither should the card be rolled up, for this practice often necessitates unrolling the notes at a critical point. Notes should never be written on large sheets of paper, for the tendency is to fold the paper while speaking and thus the notes are not ready for instant use when needed. Ink should be used in preference to pencil for a speaker often unconsciously handles his notes a good deal while speaking, and writing in pencil may easily be obliterated. It is often well to underscore the main headings so that they may stand out more plainly on the page, thus enabling a speaker to find his place more quickly.

The catch words of which the notes are made up should always contain some idea, some topic. Notes that merely give the first words of a sentence or paragraph, but do not contain an idea should be avoided. Such phrases as "It was once said," "Another thing to be considered," or "There was once," are often of no value at all to a speaker because he cannot remember the idea which they are meant to suggest. But if the topic is "Gas Stoves," such headings as "Economy of Gas" and "Ease of Manipulation," would be found of value. The notes should never be laid on the desk, for the speaker may find himself some distance from the desk just at the time when he most needs his notes, or he may be forced to bend over the desk in order to see them, thus having to take his eyes off of the audience for too long a time. If the notes are laid on the desk, and then the speaker steps out to the front of the desk, he will find that he will have to step back in order to see his notes, which also causes an awkward pause. Notes should be written, then, on cards, on one side, in writing large enough to be seen from the waist-line, and should be carried by the speaker without any effort at concealment.

Objections to the Extemporaneous Style

Numerous objections are often made to the extempore speech. It is charged that slang and colloquial expressions abound in it, that there is unnecessary repetition and diffuseness, that the sentence structure is often faulty, that the grammar is often poor, that the speaker often makes rash and ill-considered statements. All of these charges are, of course, at one time or another, justified, but these are faults in the practice of the method and not in the method itself. Persistent practice and supplementary study should be indulged in until these faults are eliminated. It takes a longer time to perfect the extemporaneous style of speaking, but the freedom and excellence which it finally gives the speaker, and even the results at earlier periods of his training, fully justify its being called the best style, all things considered.

IV. The Combination Style

Sometimes speakers use a combination of styles. A speaker may write and read in part, and speak from memory in part. Or he may write and read in some portions and extemporize in others. Or he may extemporize on the whole, but introduce portions delivered from memory. Whatever combinations of style the speaker may use, however, it will be found that the result is usually "spotty." The audience is well aware that there has been a change in style, and attention will be taken from the speech and expended upon watching the speaker and his varying methods, or the audience will pay attention to the parts it likes, which are usually the extemporized parts, and will not listen to the other parts. It is often justifiable to fix the thought of the opening sentence or two quite firmly in mind, even giving attention to the wording, and the same practice may be pursued in regard to the few closing sentences, but further than this the speaker should trust to the moment for his language.

Of all the methods of preparing and delivering a speech, then, the extemporaneous style should be the one adopted. Writing and reading, speaking from memory, speaking impromptu, and styles of speaking which involve one or more types of preparation and delivery should be avoided.

REVIEW

Question: What style are *you* going to use in *your* speaking?

Answer: The extemporaneous style (with notes, perhaps, at the start).

Now stick to it!

ASSIGNMENT

Now you know enough about speaking to *really begin in earnest.*

For your first assignment *relate some experience of yours, or explain something* with which you are familiar. Good first speeches have been made on "The Slide Rule," "A Chinese Puzzle" (explaining how it is worked), "How Shoes Are Made" (illustrating the processes from a shoe sawed in two and held in the hand) and "A Novel Filing Card" (showing the card to the audience). If you undertake to relate an experience, be sure not to make it a mere itinerary, telling when you left a certain place and when you arrived at another. *Tell what happened.* You might speak on "A Hunting Trip I Once Took" or "The Grand Canyon at Sunset." *Be simple. Do not try to do too much.*

Limit your speech to four minutes.

Use the extemporaneous style.

You may rehearse (try) the speech two or three times before you *really* give it. The language will, of course, differ on each occasion, but the path of the thought should be the same.

Read the following speech—an actual first speech of a *beginner* in public speaking.

Apricot Drying

Three or four years ago it was my privilege to spend a few weeks upon my uncle's ranch in California during the season of apricot drying, and I think that perhaps many of you—especially those who have not seen apricots being dried—will be interested in knowing just what processes are involved between the picking of the ripe apricots and the displaying of the tempting golden fruit as it lies exposed in the neighborhood grocery.

First of all, the apricot trees are not allowed to grow tall, but are made by skillful pruning to spread out over a wider area than they naturally would. This is because, if the trees are high, the men who pick the apricots from tall stepladders cannot reach the fruit so easily as if the trees are lower.

The picking is usually done by contract. The rancher signs a contract with some man —often a foreigner—who is able to control the necessary amount of labor to pick his apricots at a certain time. This man to whom the contract is let, is responsible for getting a certain number of pickers at a certain time. The pickers are paid by the box and the contractor's work is done when the apricots are in boxes on the ground in stacks.

From the stacks of boxes the apricots are taken to the cutting shed. The cutting shed is just a framework holding up a roof over the cutters to protect them from the hot sun. The cutters halve the fruit, take out the seeds, and place it upon large trays in a single layer. The cutters are paid by the number of boxes they prepare and put on the trays. As the trays are filled they are taken in stacks to the sulphur shed.

The sulphur shed is just a small shed, six or eight feet high and ten or twelve feet in length and breadth. The shed is air-tight, and when the trays are in the shed, sulphur is lighted in it and the door closed. The fruit is left in the shed for eight or ten hours, when it is taken out and laid on the ground to dry. The apricots are given the sulphur treatment for the purpose of keeping flies and other insects away from the fruit while it is drying, for no insect will touch the fruit after it has been given the sulphur-shed treatment.

When the fruit is sufficiently shriveled, the trays are stacked and left to cure for several days.

All of this work is done in the open air, for there is no danger of rain in California during the summer months.

Finally the fruit is carefully looked over, the bad fruit discarded, and the good fruit packed in boxes and put in storage for sale.

NOW, MAKE THE OUTLINE OF YOUR SPEECH

It ought to take you fifteen or twenty minutes to prepare your outline.

After you have finished your outline, go over it silently four or five times, to be sure you are familiar with it.

You will find that going over your speech *aloud* will help you greatly in selecting the proper words with which to express your thoughts, and it will also help you in *remembering your speech.*

Go completely through the speech each time, even though you do have trouble with the words, for only in this way will you be able to fix the path of your thought in mind.

After you have finished, however, you may go back and improve the parts you had trouble with. The next time you rehearse the speech you will find that these parts will not offer difficulty.

PART E

HOW TO REMEMBER A SPEECH

In *Part D* of this lesson it was stated that the use of notes during the delivery of a speech is no crime. This is true, and some of the most effective speakers use notes. However, oftentimes a speaker will do better, and feel more free, if he can dispense with notes, and it will be the purpose of this part of the lesson to point out some methods of remembering speeches.

The two great essentials of remembering are:

1st, Vivid impression, *and*

2nd, Association of impressions

If a speaker can bring these to bear upon the speech that he wishes to remember, he will have little difficulty. Here are several ways in which a speaker may do this.

FIRST: A SPEAKER MAY REMEMBER HOW HIS SPEECH-OUTLINE LOOKED ON PAPER. If a speech outline is well arranged on cards or a sheet of paper, often all that is needed is an intense contemplation of the cards or paper for a few moments. This serves to deepen the impression of the way the outline looks, and when the speaker takes his eyes off the outline a distinct image of it remains in his mind. This impression can often be still further deepened by using "display" features in preparing the outline. For example, the main heads can be underscored, or printed with a pen in larger letters than the remainder of the outline. Sometimes colored inks can be used to good advantage. In this case, the main heads may appear in black ink, the sub-heads in green ink, and the sub-sub-heads in red ink. A certain good speaker among Chicago lawyers makes out the outlines of his speeches upon large sheets of paper with a camel's-hair brush. He then looks at these outlines intently at several different times before he is to speak, and then appears before his audiences without any notes whatsoever.

SECOND: A SPEAKER MAY SEE THE THINGS HE WISHES TO TALK ABOUT JUST AS THEY WOULD APPEAR IN THE OUTSIDE WORLD. For example, if a speech is to be given on the manufacture of paper, the speaker may see in imagination the different steps as they are taken in some factory with which he is familiar. He would, in this case, see the ships come up to the dock, loaded with the rags, or old paper, or wood to be used in the manufacture of the paper. He would see this material carried to the "shredders," where it is broken up into fine pulp. Then he would see the pulp in the "mixers" where the coloring matter and other needed ingredients are added. Then he would see this finished pulp carried into the paper mill proper, and spread upon the long belts which carry it between the rollers and gradually dry and harden it until it becomes at the other end of the mill real paper wound upon large rollers. In such a speech there is no need to remember an outline on paper. The speaker can just walk through the factory (in imagination) and tell what he sees. A good speech on Efficient Gas Manufacture was once made by this method. The speaker simply described in the first part of his speech an old, inefficient, out-of-date gas plant that he had recently visited, and followed this description with a description of a modern, efficient, up-to-date gas plant that he had recently seen.

THIRD: A SPEAKER MAY USE SHORT WORD HEADINGS ALL BEGINNING WITH THE SAME LETTER. Such an outline could be used for a talk on electric refrigeration. A speaker in a talk on this subject might wish to bring out the following points:

The temperature in an electric refrigerator is lower than that in an ordinary ice refrigerator.

The electric refrigerator preserves food better than the ordinary ice refrigerator.

The temperature is more constant.

There is no anxiety lest the ice melt before the ice-man comes.

There is no bother with carrying ice into the kitchen, and thus getting kitchen floor covered with drippings from the ice and with dirt from the ice-man's shoes.

The electric refrigerator is more economical than the ordinary ice refrigerator.

These topics could be further grouped under three main heads in this fashion:

Temperature Cleanliness Economy

But even this outline would not be found so easy to remember as the following:

Cold	Care
Conserves	Clean
Constant	Cost

If the speaker would say such an outline as this over again and again, he would be very likely to have no difficulty in remembering his speech.

FOURTH: A SPEAKER MAY CONSTRUCT A SENTENCE, EACH WORD OF WHICH WILL SUGGEST A HEADING IN HIS SPEECH. For example, if a speech were to be made on the subject of personality, and a speaker wished to bring out the qualities that go to make up a good personality, he could use these qualities:

Friendship	Earnestness
Sympathy	A clear conscience
Physical well-being	

These could be remembered by the following sentence:

*F*ellows *S*ucceed *E*xceptionally who *C*onsider *P*ersonality.

Here "Fellows" begins with an F, and so does Friendship. "Succeed" begins with an S, and so does Sympathy. "Exceptionally" begins with an E and so does Earnestness. "Consider" begins with a C, and so does Conscience. "Personality" begins with a P, and so does Physical well-being. Thus a speaker should have no trouble remembering his outline.

FIFTH: A SPEAKER MAY CONSTRUCT A FANTASTIC MENTAL PICTURE, THE VARIOUS FEATURES OF WHICH WILL SUGGEST THE HEADINGS IN HIS OUTLINE. Suppose a speaker wishes to speak on "Modern Business Methods" and wishes to treat these topics:

Organization	Advertising
Co-operation	Salesmanship

In such a case, he could first picture a pipe-organ. This would suggest "Organization." Then he could have several men cooperating in repairing the organ—one man working on the keyboard, another on the pedals, a third on the motor, and a fourth painting the pipes. These men, working together, would suggest "Co-operation." "Advertising" could be suggested by having the sign "Use Sherwin-Williams Paints" painted on the backs of the white coats of the men. "Salesmanship" could be suggested by having a travelling salesman (with sample case and travelling bag, just stepping off a passenger coach) appear just below the slogan "Use Sherwin-Williams Paints." Thus by seeing this complete picture of the organ, with the men co-operating, and with the Sherwin-Williams "ad" and the picture of the travelling salesman appearing on their white coats, the whole outline could be remembered.

It may be said, however, that often if as much time is given to remembering the outline itself as to constructing such a picture, the speaker will have no difficulty.

SIXTH: A SPEAKER MAY OFTEN "HANG" HIS OUTLINE ON SOME WELL-KNOWN PHRASE. Thus, a speech on "Democracy" could be hung on Lincoln's well-known phrase, "government of the people, by the people, and for the people."

NOTE: As a speaker progresses in the art of speaking, he will find himself depending less and less upon these devices and more and more upon the *logical connection* of his topics. This is because he is less and less disturbed by the sensation of speaking and because his mind becomes more and more accustomed to thinking logically. *Care should always be taken to make the outline as logical as possible,* for then there is less possibility of forgetting.

After a speaker has constructed his outline in such a way that he can easily remember it, the development of the various topics is best remembered by frequent mental and oral rehearsals. The actual thinking through of the speech, *all the thoughts being put into words,* will tend to impress the speech upon the mind, and the actual *whispering* or *saying aloud* of the speech will help even more.

Effective Speech

MANUAL II

SPEAKING ON SPECIAL OCCASIONS

TABLE OF CONTENTS

MANUAL II

MANUAL II

HOW TO PRESENT A GIFT
HOW TO ACCEPT A GIFT
HOW TO ACCEPT AN OFFICE
HOW TO MAKE AN ANNOUNCEMENT

This manual will have to do with four kinds of speeches that are very common. They are not strictly *business speeches,* but they are speeches that almost anyone may be called upon to make in the course of his *social life,* and it is often through the impression that a man makes on such occasions as these that he adds to his influence in his business relations and in his community life.

Further they are easy speeches to make, and can at once be put to use.

No speaker can hope to attain success unless he does much speaking, and every man ambitious for success should begin his speaking before actual audiences without delay.

Study these types of speeches, therefore, carefully, and then accept the first opportunity that comes your way to make use of them.

PRESENTING A GIFT

In *this* lesson I am going to tell you first of all *how to Present a Gift.*

Now, of course, you may present a gift to *one* person before a *few friends,* or you may present a gift to *a lodge, a club, a school, a church or a college or university,* or any other organization or institution, before a large audience.

When you present a gift to one person you should make your speech

1. Genial
2. Kindly
3. Appreciative

Do you know what is meant by *genial?*

Just to save time, I am going to tell you a few things that the dictionary says it means.

First, it means (in the case of soil, or climate) *favorable to growth or comfort.* Hence we say a *genial soil,* or a *genial climate.* Can you make your speech favorable to the growth (spiritual and material) of the person to whom you are to present the gift?

Again, the dictionary says that genial means *contributing to and sympathizing with the enjoyment of life.* Can you make your speech *contribute to the enjoyment of life by the person to whom you present the gift?* Can you make it contribute to the enjoyment of life *by those present to hear you?*

Here are some other things that the dictionary says *genial* means. It means *jovial.* Can you make your speech jovial? It means *exciting pleasure and sympathy.* Can you in your speech *excite the pleasure* of the person to whom you give the gift? Can you *excite the pleasure* of those of the friends who are present? Can you *create a feeling of sympathy* among the friends for the failures and *especially* the *successes* of the one whom you are honoring? To be *genial* further means *enlivening.* Can you *enliven* the party (be the "life of the party"!) in your speech?

Do you know what *kindly* means?

Well, here are a few synonyms from the dictionary:

Benevolent	Humane
Benign	Compassionate
Beneficent	Good
Bounteous	Lenient
Gracious	Clement
Propitious	Mild
Generous	Gentle
Forbearing	Bland
Indulgent	Obliging
Tender	Friendly

Just think what a field here opens for you!

Do you know what *appreciative* means?

The dictionary says to *appreciate* means to *estimate justly,* to *set a value on,* to *recognize or feel the worth of,* to *esteem duly.*

Can you do these things with your friend?

Well, you now know something, at least, as to what kind of a speech you should make.

NOTE: I have taken this much time to point out the real meanings of *genial, kindly,* and *appreciative,* in order to show *one* way by which any person *who really desires to become a good speaker* may secure help. Remember always:

THE DICTIONARY IS THE SPEAKER'S BEST FRIEND

Now suppose you are to present a small gift to Mr. Jones.

Here are a few things you may say!

SUGGESTIVE OUTLINE FOR THE PRESENTATION OF A PERSONAL GIFT

1. Tell Mr. Jones you have been selected to present him with a token of friendship and esteem
2. Tell him something about the gift
   (*a*) What it is—its usefulness—its beauty.
   (*b*) Any particular feature about the gift that is worthy of note

3. Tell him this gift, however, is not given for itself, but as an expression of
   - (*a*) Love for a trusted friend
   - (*b*) Respect for true leadership
   - (*c*) Gratitude for service rendered, such as
     - (1) Breaking a record
     - (2) Showing how well a task can be performed
     - (3) Giving real inspiration
4. Tell him you hope the gift will often bring back happy memories

If you can introduce a little *humor* in your speech, it will be welcome. On the other hand do not neglect *true sentiment.* "The smile that shines through tears" is often the note that will find most ready response.

NOTE: Not all the headings given in the *Suggestive Outline* need be given, and the *order need not be closely adhered to,* and they may be *fully developed or briefly stated as the occasion demands.*

FOR THE LARGER OCCASION

If the gift is presented in the presence of an audience of considerable size, the outline still holds good, but the presentation takes on a little more dignity.

The following examples will serve to illustrate the usual procedure.

PRESENTATION OF A SILVER SERVICE

TO JOHN H. PUELICHER

Retiring President of the American Bankers Association

BY THOMAS B. MCADAMS

(Speech delivered before the American Bankers Association Convention.)

To awaken the banker to a clearer conception of his opportunities for leadership, to educate broadly that truth rather than prejudice may determine the actions of individuals and the policies of government, to stimulate the desire for generous service in behalf of the national welfare, to discourage movements for unsound legislation or administration, conceived in selfishness and advocated in the interest of organized minorities, to stimulate individual initiative and protest against governmental interference with the proper development of private enterprise, to develop in our people a grateful appreciation for the privileges of American citizenship, with the accompanying responsibility to protect unsullied and unspoiled those fundamental principles upon which our history is founded—to these practical problems the energy and ability of the administration now drawing to a close was devoted, with an earnestness and fearlessness which commanded the admiration and respect of every American banker.

To commemorate the vitality of your administration, Mr. Puelicher, and to remind you constantly that, in addition to our appreciation for duty well done, we have the privilege of knowing you for what you are—this token of our good-will is now presented. In your year of unselfish service in behalf of banking and the protection of the fundamentals of American society, the theories of an educator, the dreams of a poet, the soul of a musician, have enabled you to see truly great visions, which the practical viewpoint and experience of the trained banker—combined with the character and fearlessness of real manhood—have privileged you to convert into far-seeing policies and definite action.

Great achievements are necessarily based upon great motives. For the source of your inspiration we turn to the words of Kipling:

> And only the Master shall praise us
> And only the Master shall blame,
> And no one shall work for money,
> And no one shall work for fame.

But each for the joy of the working,
And each in his separate star,
Shall draw the thing as he sees it,
For the God of Things as They Are.

May the God of things as they are ever guide and protect you in your years of further service for Him and humanity.

PRESENTATION OF SERVICE PINS TO EMPLOYEES OF THE FULLER BRUSH COMPANY

BY

A. A. WHETSTONE

Educational Director of the Fuller Brush Company

(Speech delivered at a convention of employees of The Fuller Brush Company at the Key Route Inn, Oakland, California.)

Perhaps some do not realize the significance of these service pins which are about to be presented to these men. Four or five years ago we got to talking about some recognized emblem we could give the men working for us, and we thought of the stripes on the train men, and of the different ways in which different companies give their men recognition for service. Finally we decided on these emblems.

This emblem is given to the Fuller Brush Company men to show appreciation of especially good work done. This emblem cannot be bought with money, nor is it ever sold at any price; the only way it can be got is by faithful service. It stands for character, and it stands for unconquerable spirit. It is a mark of esteem which the Company bestows in appreciation of the excellent service the men have given to the Company.

Each year of service the men are presented with a pin showing the length of time they have been with us, and at the end of five years a pin with a diamond in it is presented to them. Then it is replaced after another five years with a pin having two diamonds in it.

I want to congratulate these men on having performed the service which makes Mr. Fuller proud. It is a pleasure for me to present these pins in the name of our President, Mr. Fuller, for it is his idea to show in this way the loyalty of these men. I hope that all of them will keep on working until they all wear diamonds, and many diamonds.

PRESENTING A GIFT TO AN ORGANIZATION OR INSTITUTION

When a gift is to be presented to an organization or institution, the following outline will be found of use. This outline, like the one just given for the presentation of a personal gift, may be changed at will to suit the occasion. Topics may be omitted, or new ones added, as the speaker may deem fit. However, the usual procedure is about as indicated in the outline.

Suggestive Outline for the Presentation of a Gift to an Organization or Institution

A. State the general purpose of the gathering

B. Talk a little while about the gift itself

1. What it is
2. How it differs from other gifts
3. Its history
4. How the funds for its purchase were procured
5. How the idea of its presentation originated

C. Tell why it is given

1. Its usefulness
    a. The needs of the institution
    b. How the gift meets the needs of the institution

2. Its beauty
    a. The intrinsic beauty of the gift
    b. Its appropriateness to its surroundings
3. Its spiritual value
    a. To give convincing and tangible expression to the feelings of the givers (and for their sakes), such as
        (1) Their love
        (2) Their respect
        (3) Their gratitude
        (4) Their memory of happy associations
    b. (If in memory of an event) To perpetuate the memory of the event in the honor of which the gift is made
        (1) The characteristics of the event
        (2) The significance of the event
    c. (If in memory of a person) To perpetuate the memory of the person in whose honor the gift is made
        (1) The character of the person
        (2) His deeds
        (3) The significance of his life

D. Express the hope that the gift will fulfill its mission

Here is an example of the speech presenting a gift to a great industrial organization.

PRESENTATION OF A STATUE OF HENRY J. HEINZ

TO THE H. J. HEINZ COMPANY

By Howard Heinrich

Representing the Employees of the H. J. Heinz Company

(Speech delivered at Pittsburgh, Pennsylvania, on the occasion of the eightieth anniversary of the birth of Henry J. Heinz, the founder of the H. J. Heinz Company, and the fifty-fifth anniversary of the establishment of the business.)

This is a significant and impressive hour. Summoned by the memories of him whom we "have loved long since and lost awhile," we assemble here to pay our tributes of respect and affection, and from a life so nobly lived, so surely crowned, to get incentive and inspiration for the brief span of years that yet remains to us.

Following the death of the founder of H. J. Heinz Company, which occurred on the fourteenth day of May, 1919, the employees of the Company, whom he loved and by whom he was loved, sought some means whereby they might express to the Company and the world their respect and affection for him, who was their friend.

They sought something that could be associated with the business, so daily contact with it would remind them of his life and work and character. They wanted something that would keep alive in their memories the outlines of the familiar form and figure, surmounted by the noble brow, and with smiling countenance illumined by the sparkling but kindly eyes. They desired something that should be enduring, typical of his influence upon their lives and upon the business which he, as leader, with their loyal co-operation as followers, had created. What could more completely meet these requirements than his statue, in enduring bronze, to stand in some suitable place on the premises?

It was so decided. Every employee in the service of the Company, when the earthly life of the founder closed, voluntarily and lovingly contributed to a fund with which to procure the statue. Mr. Emil Fuchs of New York, artist and sculptor, was commissioned to create this employees' memorial, and we assemble here today, October 11, 1924, on the eightieth anniversary of the founder's birth, to unveil it, and to present it to the Company.

But before this is done, why, may I ask, were the employees of this Company prompted to do this thing? For what reason did they give him loyalty, love and devotion in life, and why do they now perpetuate his memory in this enduring form?

In the first place, he was their friend. He had a great capacity for friendship. They never doubted the sincerity and genuineness of it. In the next place, he was a fair employer. He made a fair bargain—one the benefits of which were mutual, for he believed the bargain with unequal benefits was not only futile, but immoral. Having made a fair bargain, he stood ready to perform his part, not alone in letter, but in spirit, and he demanded like conduct on the part of the other. If causes beyond control made that bargain inequitable, he was quick to volunteer relief through a suitable modification.

He was kind, he was thoughtful, he was considerate—but it is in something more than all these things that the reason for this memorial is to be found.

It is to be found in the kind of a man he was and in the kind of a life he lived. The chief elements of his strength were his moral character and his religious earnestness. He reached his port by toil, by eyes uplifted to the stars, and by the daily grip of God's strong hand. It is character that counts in the great crises of life. Far above his ability as a captain of industry, above his skill in business, above his extensive information and well-reasoned convictions on life in general, the great strength of Henry John Heinz was in that patience and far vision and confident faith which grew out of his moral convictions and dependence on the source of all power. So through the stormy years when the business he had founded (and there were years of stress and storm) was feeling its way along and slowly finding itself, and through the more favored seas into which it came, where the sunshine of prosperity rested upon it, Henry J. Heinz, with great ability, with great labor, with great patience, and most of all, with great faith, in himself, in his fellow man, in his God, and in the eternal principles of righteousness, kept a steady hand in the helm.

One who sees with his faith as well as with his eyes, has a peace, a confidence, an inspiration denied to others. It was so with him.

Mr. Heinz was a prophet. He saw great things ahead. His thought moved in spacious realms, with a largeness of conception that made him a striking character in any conference. He thought in "totals" not in "items." His daring was both challenging and contagious. He was a great teacher. He ever sought to impart to others any truth by which he had come through toil and experience. Best of all his works was the training of his successors. He built for the future.

His example still speaks. He is speaking to us today, to those who were his business associates for many years, and to those who never saw or met him, but recognize that his was the life of character, of conscience, and of brotherly kindness.

Standing here before his unveiled statue, in the presence of those who knew him and loved him, may I offer in words written of another, but appropriate to him, this ode:

TO THE FOUNDER

'Tis one thing that the deeds you wrought have brought success, and given man his due.
It is another when a master's hand has builded better than he knew.
You built so that success did crown your efforts as you guided deed or act
But to lay plans that others, coming on, might shape a fancy into fact
Is better still. And praise unmeasured unto masters of this class is due—
And on your tomb might be this epitaph: A man who builded better than he knew.

Mr. Heinz, in behalf of the employees of H. J. Heinz Company, in token of the exalted place which the founder holds in their interest and affection, and whose place in their hearts is firmly fixed, I present to the Company this memorial of the founder.

The fragrance of his life still abides to inspire others as he inspired, to serve as he served. The years will not dim his memory.

ACCEPTING A GIFT

And now I shall tell you *How to Accept a Gift.*

Here is a suggestive outline for the *Acceptance of a Personal Gift.*

Suggestive Outline for the Acceptance of a Personal Gift

A. Formally state your acceptance of the gift, stating
   1. Your surprise (if any) at
      (*a*) Receiving any gift at all, *or*
      (*b*) Receiving this particular gift, *or*
   2. Your pleasure in
      (*a*) Receiving this token of affection, expressing
         (1) Confidence
         (2) Good will
         (3) Esteem
         (4) Love, etc.
      (*b*) Receiving this particular gift
         (1) of such usefulness (tell of its uses)

(2) of such beauty (point out its beauties)

(3) of such touching associations (recount them)

B. Express any particular sentiments that lie close to your heart

C. Thank the givers of the gift

(*a*) for the gift itself

(*b*) for the spirit behind the gift

(1) its generosity

(2) its affection

(3) its loyalty, etc.

The speech of acceptance is really the counterpart or reciprocal of the speech of presentation, and should be "dovetailed" into the speech of presentation that has been given. The speaker should "pick up" any particularly striking remarks of the preceding speaker and use them to his advantage. Not all the headings given in the preceding outline will always appear in the speech and the order in which they appear may often be changed.

(Although in the speech of Mr. Stillwell, which follows, there is no mention of the traveling bag and cuff links, doubtless there was some informal mention of them either at the beginning or end of the speech.)

Here is an example of a Speech of Acceptance.

ACCEPTANCE OF TRAVELING BAG AND CUFF LINKS

By Giles H. Stillwell

Past President of the Chamber of Commerce, Syracuse, New York

(Speech delivered at a Chamber of Commerce Luncheon at Syracuse, New York, upon the presentation of a traveling bag and cuff links by the members of the chamber, to the speaker, who was retiring from the presidency.)

The city of Syracuse owes me nothing. If accounts were balanced at this date, I would be the debtor. Haven't I, all these years, lived within the limits of the city and shared all its benefits? Haven't I had the benefit of its schools, churches and hospitals? Haven't I had the use of its library, parks and public places? Haven't I had the protection of its fire, police and health departments? Haven't its people, during all this time, been gathering for me, from the four corners of the earth, food for my table, clothing for my body and material for my home? Hasn't the city furnished the patronage by which I have succeeded in my profession? Has it not furnished the best friends of my life, whose ideals have been my inspiration, whose kind words have been my cheer and whose helpfulness has carried me over my greatest difficulties? What shall I give in return? Not simply taxes which cover so small a part of what I have received. I want to give more. I want, of my own free will, to give enough so that I can rightfully say, "This is my city." So that I can take pride in "my city"; so that I can take pride in its prosperity, in the honors that come to its citizens and in all that makes it greater and better. I can do this only by becoming a part of the city, by giving to it generously of myself. In this way only can I, even in small part, pay the great debt I owe to Syracuse. In the Chamber of Commerce I have my chance and I believe in it.

Here is a suggestive outline for a speech *Accepting a Gift for an Institution or Organization.*

Suggestive Outline for a Speech Accepting a Gift for an Institution or Organization

1. Formally state your acceptance of the gift, stating
   - (*a*) What it is
     - (1) How it differs from other gifts
     - (2) Its history
     - (3) How the funds for purchase were procured

(4) How the idea of its presentation originated

(*b*) By whom it is accepted

(*c*) From whom it is accepted

2. State the significance of the gift

(*a*) Its usefulness

(1) The needs of the recipient

(2) How the gift meets the needs of the recipient

(*b*) Its beauty

(*c*) Its spiritual value

(1) To those who have it

(*x*) As an expression of their spirit

(*y*) As a fit climax to effort

(2) To those who accept it

(*x*) As a tribute

(*m*) To themselves and their work

(*n*) To the one honored (This may be developed in detail)

(*y*) As an inspiration

(*m*) To all those in any way related to the institution involved

(*n*) To posterity

3. Thank the givers and give assurance that the gift will be sacredly treasured.

Study carefully the following speech, comparing it with the *Suggestive Outline*.

ACCEPTANCE OF A STATUE OF HENRY J. HEINZ

BY HOWARD HEINZ

Director of the H. J. Heinz Company

(Speech delivered at Pittsburgh, Pennsylvania, on the occasion of the eightieth anniversary of the birth of Henry J. Heinz, the founder of the H. J. Heinz Company, and the fifty-fifth anniversary of the establishment of the business.)

On this great day in the history of our business when we celebrate fifty-five years of mutual good will between employer and employees, we have no more sacred duty than to set this hour apart in which to reverently and gratefully acknowledge, not only this splendid gift, but the more splendid life of him who remains with us in precious memory.

Your spokesman has beautifully referred to some of the marks of the man whose memory we have met to honor. Those here who did not know the founder may deem those words fulsome and extravagant praise, but those of us who knew him and worked with him, know how completely and faithfully they speak the truth. During his lifetime, we counted his friendship as one of our most precious possessions and the recollection of our intercourse with him will always be one of our most cherished memories. As a son, with the intimate knowledge which that relationship affords, I can say, and I say it with pride and reverence, he was one of those few great men who do not grow smaller the nearer you approach them. He was possessed with the greatest industry. He was tireless and indefatigable. He was not too big for little things. He was simple in his tastes and the habits of his life; strong in his convictions. He received with deference advice and suggestions and, while ever confident of his own judgment, was devoid of arrogance. He was as gleeful as the little children for whom he had so much love and many of whom in one way or another were the objects of his bounty. At his mother's knee he learned the lesson of reverence for the Bible and built his life upon faith in its message. That faith produced in him that cheerful, happy optimism that made him courageous in times of discouragement. He had the personal charm of winning others to his own optimism. It was both infectious and contagious.

Successful in business, devoted to the church, loyal to his country and the welfare of its people, a more marked characteristic was his interest in the individual man, woman and child. He was always busy rendering service in a personal way as if he thought his supreme duty lay in the needs of the particular person at the moment. His business, his life, his associations and his activities were never so important as to interfere with his personal service to people in the humblest stations in life.

But his place in the history of this business is secure. Nothing that we can do or say can exalt it or diminish it. Its value to us who came after him and to those who shall come after us is in his example and in the inspiration of his life.

In the presence of this splendid and beautiful memorial—the founder's statue, so true to life in poise and features and smile, and the two bas-reliefs, symbolizing the dominant traits of his life—industry and religion, love of achievement and love of fellow men—what is the lesson we should learn?

Is it not a lesson of making our lives count? Many of us here have advantages superior to those he enjoyed. What will we do with them? It is very apparent that we are not all equally gifted. There are wide differences in gifts, as regards intellectual and spiritual capacity, but every one of us is responsible for making his life count in the best way and to the best end. He is a failure who refuses to strive earnestly because he knows some-one else will excel him. The founder was never discouraged or restrained by such a thought. It is not a disgrace to be a one talent man. It is a disgrace to fail to make faithful use of that talent. It is astonishing what results may be achieved with ordinary resources when there are added industry, patience, faith and consecration to life's purposes. The founder's life is an example of this. It is essential that there be a whole-hearted dedication to high and noble purposes if our lives are to count for most. That is what this life of which we are now thinking teaches. Unless we learn this lesson, this hour, this presentation, this dedication might just as well not have been.

No tribute of the employees could have touched my heart more tenderly or deeply than their desire to perpetuate my father's memory and influence, as their spokesman has told us. Their spontaneous, voluntary offerings to the fund to provide this memorial which we dedicate today filled my heart with gratitude, and the directors of the Company are equally appreciative with me. It gives me the greatest pleasure and the utmost satisfaction, Mr. Heinrich, to accept, in the name of H. J. Heinz Company from you and from all of the employees whom you represent, this very beautiful memorial gift. We are happy to have this memento of his face and of his figure. We do not need it for ourselves, for loving memory will not let us forget them, but if our successors want to know the kind of a man whose labor built this institution, whose genius led it to prosperity, whose inspiration has endowed us to carry it on and whose influence still exerts itself in its councils, your gift today has made it possible.

So, speaking for myself as well as for my fellow-directors, I desire now, through you, most heartily to thank the employees for their beautiful and appropriate gift. In thus honoring the founder, I believe you have honored yourselves.

ACCEPTING AN OFFICE

When you have heard the cry "Speech! Speech!" from a crowd of your friends after you have been elected to office you have doubtless been "almost paralyzed."

You need no longer be!

Here are a few things you may say!

Suggestive Outline for a Speech Accepting an Office

1. Thank your friends for having honored you by electing you to the office
2. Tell them you realize the responsibility falling upon one who is to follow such officers as have previously held this office, stating
   (*a*) Their talents
   (*b*) Their faithfulness to duty
   (*c*) Their sacrifices
3. Tell them you are sorry (if this is the general sentiment abroad) that the officers of the last year could not continue in office
   (*a*) Because of the constitutional provision (if any) that no officer shall hold office more than one term
   (*b*) Because ill health has prevented them from continuing in office
   (*c*) Because business necessity has compelled resignation, etc.
4. Tell them you will do your best to carry on the traditions of the organization
5. Tell them some of the things you hope to do

6. Express confidence in the loyalty of the membership and their willingness to cooperate
7. Assert your own loyalty to the organization and repeat the fact that you will do all in your power to make the coming year a prosperous one for the organization

Here are the mental notes you can carry in your mind, *not on paper,* in preparing this speech.

I. Thanks
II. Realize responsibility
III. Regret previous administration
IV. Will do best
V. Mean to do (certain things)
VI. Confidence in members
VII. Do all in my power

You can remember the *first three points* by remembering T. R. (Theodore Roosevelt). You can remember points IV an V by remembering W. M. (William McKinley). You can remember the last two points by remembering C. & D. (Coolidge and Dawes). If you will say

Theodore Roosevelt
William McKinley
Coolidge and Dawes

over and over, you cannot forget your speech. Try such a system as this for remembering many of your speeches.

NOTICE THIS

The speech of acceptance by a newly elected officer of an organization is *an important matter* to him. By his speech he will either live up to the hopes that his associates have reposed in him and thus give his administration a good beginning, or he will fail to do this and thus handicap all his later efforts.

Do Not Hurt Anyone's Feelings

Consequently, a newly elected officer should be particularly careful not to hurt *anyone's* feelings. *The shortcomings of the previous administration should not be mentioned,* and, as far as possible, the *outgoing officers should be complimented.* The loyalty of *all* the members of an organization is necessary to a successful carrying on of the year's work, and the loyalty *even of those who have opposed the incoming officer* should be sought.

The policies outlined for the ensuing year should be expressed clearly and optimistically. The power of the new administration will largely be judged by the *broad common sense,* the *clarity* and the *energy,* of the successful candidate in his speech of acceptance. Yet there must be a *balance* between *power* and modesty. Too great modesty will leave an impression of weakness, but too much assertiveness will leave an impression of egotism and will antagonize many in the organization.

REMEMBER THIS

Any member of an organization that feels there is *any possibility* of his being elected to office at a coming meeting *should prepare a speech of acceptance beforehand.* True, this speech may never be delivered, but, at any rate, the speaker will be prepared and "you'd be surprised" at how many speeches of this sort, prepared beforehand, *have never been given!* Be ready! It is not egotistic to prepare for unforeseen circumstances. It is just *plain common sense!*

THE ACCEPTANCE OF AN OFFICE OFTEN TAKES THE FORM OF AN INAUGURAL SPEECH

Often the speech of a newly elected officer is delayed until the time when he first presides over the organization. In such cases, the speech assumes greater formality and dignity, although the *outline of the speech remains about the same.*

Study carefully the following speech and compare it with the outline already given.

INAUGURAL ADDRESS

AS PRESIDENT OF THE KIWANIS CLUB OF PITTSBURGH, PENNSYLVANIA

BY HENRY RUSSELL MILLER

(Speech delivered at Pittsburgh, Pennsylvania.)

The time of the passing of the gavel is a significant one in the life of any such club, not merely because of our regret at the passing of a well tried and well loved leadership, not even because of the problem which a new and untried man always presents, but because the moment points a wholesome truth —which your new officers will do well always to keep in mind—that no one man is essential to the life of this club, that Kiwanis is bigger than any one man. Directors and officers may come and go, but Kiwanis goes on, always a bigger, finer, more splendid thing.

I say that sincerely. Yet I cannot let this opportunity pass to express the regret which I share with you that Dave Murdoch's term has expired. His leadership I have admired, respected and gladly followed; and to his faithful, always fine-spirited and sometimes self-sacrificing service to Kiwanis I bear witness from a full heart. I should be failing in a pleasant duty also if I did not pay tribute to three valued directors whose terms have now expired. We recognize the wisdom of rotation in office, and we welcome the new directors gladly, but we are reconciled to the passing of Phil Freyvogel, Sam Kekilty and Jim Bunting from the board only because we know we shall always have their loyal friendship and co-operation.

Pittsburgh Kiwanis consists not of a board of directors merely, but of a membership of some three hundred men.

You have, as responsible directors of the club activities, eleven men of your own choosing. They will give you the best they have. In return, they ask the full, wholehearted co-operation of the entire membership. We take office, deeply conscious that this will be the critical year in the life of Pittsburgh Kiwanis, during which success or failure will depend, not upon what the board does or does not do, but upon the spirit, interest and activity of every man on the roster.

I said—"a critical year." During the past three years Pittsburgh Kiwanis, keeping step with the international movement, has grown apace: in numbers, certainly; in spirit, I believe; toward definition of purpose, perhaps. We have reached that point at which every such club must arrive sooner or later, a point to which—*but not beyond which*—a club can be carried by the momentum of an initial enthusiasm; a point from which it is hard to go forward but very, very easy to go back. You will understand that we must either go forward or go back. There is no such thing as standing still; when a club ceases to grow, it begins to die. When I speak of growth, I have in mind not merely numbers. While I believe we can and ought to be 500 strong, I hold numbers as unimportant. I would rather see a club of 100 genuinely sold on Kiwanis than one of 500 to whom it is but a pleasant but insignificant incident. I speak rather of growth in character, in effective influence upon the membership and upon the community. And that can be achieved only by a constant deepening Kiwanis consciousness in the membership. And by that I mean a serious acceptance of Kiwanis, not as a casual thing to be lightly enjoyed and as lightly esteemed, but an important principle of life—especially a spirit

—to be served, conserved and spread abroad through the community. Kiwanis is not worth the time, money and energy of busy men it consumes, if it does not take character as a compact brotherhood of serious men, strong in mutual confidence and understanding, imbued with the real community spirit, having no set program but able to make its influence felt at any given point or time, radiating at all times—first upon the membership, then upon the community—the spirit of friendly service. And he is no true Kiwanis who has not this at heart as his club's objective, plus a deep personal determination that that objective shall be reached.

The genius of Kiwanis is friendship. We call ourselves builders. I confess to a doubt that Kiwanis will ever build very much of a strictly material nature. That is not to belittle Kiwanis. The most important factors in life are the so-called "imponderables"—love and hate, truth and falsity, envy and charity, loyalty and treachery. The material things are but the instruments upon which these imponderables play. Kiwanis' first and most important contribution to the membership, the community and the world must always be spiritual.

If I had to define Kiwanis, I should do it very simply—as a concerted movement to deepen and strengthen the spirit of friendship among men. That sounds almost childishly simple. It is not simple in the sense of easy achievement or limited application. It is simple only in the sense that all fundamental things are simple. And this thing is basic.

There is a saying that a man never makes new friends after he has passed thirty. That is not literally true. But it is true that the modern struggle for success, for existence, draws a man more and more in upon himself; so that for him the world becomes a steadily narrowing circle of which he, his interests and his purposes are the center, strangling generous impulse, shutting off his view of humanity, limiting sympathy, squeezing his soul dry, until he too often becomes that most pitiable of all creatures, an utterly self-conscious, self-centered man who thinks only in terms of himself, strives only for himself, has no standards but those of selfishness. That is spiritual death.

Occasionally some great dramatic calamity such as a world war, breaks down that vicious circle for a brief moment; and a few men are born with such rare quality of soul that for them the circle never exists. But for the average man the only hope of escape from his circle is through his own conscious effort, through constant watchfulness, faithful practice in friendship, in thought for others. Kiwanis does not break down that circle, but it does something better—gives a man a chance to break through himself. It brings a man in contact with chosen men of his own sort, brings them together in conscious fellowship, says to them—"Come, my friends, out of your circle. Bring your souls into the sunlight. Here is friendship—share it if you will." This is, and must ever be, the prime function of Kiwanis. The other things we do—the speeches we hear, telling us of the world outside of our circle, the honor we pay to lonely old men who have greatly served, our kindly thought for little ones born into misfortune—these are not club objectives; they are *results of objectives attained,* the natural expression of a spirit we have either found originally or had renewed here in our Kiwanis fellowship. And as our Kiwanis consciousness deepens, those generous impulses come more often, our deeds of good will multiply.

We want to make Kiwanis such that many men will want to come in and share the gracious thing we have found. But your board cannot achieve that of itself; we need the help of the entire membership. And so we ask your whole-hearted support. First of all, in the matter of attendance. Any man some time will find it impossible to come, but most of us can be present ninety per cent of the time if only we plan for it. Never think you will not be missed. We need your presence. It helps to create atmosphere, adds to the spirit of our luncheons, gives inspiration to members and to speakers alike. No speaker is at his best when speaking to empty tables, and if we would secure speakers of the caliber we want, we must provide an audience proportioned to their talents. Moreover, you need to come. He who would have friends must show himself friendly. How can you get anything out of Kiwanis, or give anything to Kiwanis, unless you come to Kiwanis?

We ask the support of your faithful, intelligent committee service. Our committees are designed, not as empty honors, but to round out the life of the club.

But especially we ask the support of your interest and friendly understanding. Your new board is going to give, as your boards in the past have given, the best it has. What we do you shall know, and it will be done having in view the interest and desire of the club as a whole, as we know it. Now no board can please all the members all the time. Occasionally a man has some pet scheme or policy to which much brooding gives great importance in his eyes; and if it be rejected, he feels aggrieved. Beware of bitterness! It is scarcely probable, but it is at least theoretically possible, that your board some time may make a mistake; in which case we confidently expect to hear about it. Beware of bad temper! We hear it said sometimes that a friendly contest is good for a club. And that is true, provided it be a *friendly* contest, and provided both victor and loser bear themselves with good sportsmanship. To my knowledge there have been in this club contests in which the losers, by their fine spirit, have endeared themselves to the whole membership. We hear it said also that criticism is a wholesome thing, as proving interest and vitality in a club. And that too is true, *provided* the criticism be well considered from the point of view of the club as a whole, and *provided* it be frankly uttered first to the object of the criticism, in good temper and with friendly manner. Where criticism is merely the result or voice of personal bad feeling, then it is un-Kiwanian, does harm to the club and no good to the critic.

We want your suggestions as well as the support of your activity. But, while we do not expect immunity from criticism, we do ask you to believe that, where the responsibility of decision rests with the board, it is moved only by thought for the club, with unfriendliness toward none and good will to all.

I come back to what I said a moment ago —the genius of Kiwanis is friendship. If that be not true, then Kiwanis, without definite program, with no specific functions, has no important reason for existence. If that be true, then cliques, isolated groups, factionalism have no place in Kiwanis. If I can enter this room at peace with every man in it, if I can clasp hands with any other member in honest good fellowship, if I can sit at any table and say in my heart, "To every man at this table I am a friend," I have not qualified for the angelic choir— I have but done the first and simple duty of a true Kiwanian. If I sow dissension, if I keep not a guard upon my lips that I whisper no evil of any member, if I have aught of grudge or any manner of ill-feeling against any other member, and cast it not out, then the truth of Kiwanis is not in me—I am in Kiwanis, but not of it. The cardinal sin against Kiwanis is bad feeling. I do not think that in this club we have greatly sinned in this regard, but I do believe that in the critical year which we enter today, we must be specially on guard against that very thing. And so, if you have cherished any envy or jealousy or resentment against any member, I bid you, for the sake of Kiwanis, most of all for your own sake—cast it out. May this be a truly Kiwanis year, the friendliest year we have ever known.

I have said a good deal of friendship today. I have said it sincerely. Every man in this club is worthy the respect and interest of every other member. I take Kiwanis seriously because I believe that men everywhere are worthy our friendly interest; because I see a growing tendency, inevitable result of the struggle for success in our modern, complex world, a tendency that must be combated—to look upon man as a low creature, driven by base motives toward little, unworthy ends. I hate this damned cynicism, and when I see a man professing or practicing upon it, I have the measure of his soul.

Once, when under circumstances vastly different from this I was tempted to this cynicism, for my own support I wrote down a confession of my faith. Let me repeat it —I think it fits in here as I bring this talk to a close:

I consider my neighbor, weak often, erring sometimes, yet patient in failure, steadfast in toil, giving himself without stint that his children may begin one step beyond where he began. I consider my community, a million souls, toiling, striving, spending themselves that the world may be girt in steel, build bigger and stronger for generations yet to come. And when the evil is measured and the good is counted, I find that the balance is right, and I have faith.

I consider my nation, its influence a blessing, its purpose honest, its history wrought in honor, its people not weak in failure nor sodden in success. I see a field of battle, its sons—not the brilliant, not the favored, not the strong of the land only, but weakling and outcast, gathered from byway and hedge—at command of something they could not have explained but dimly saw and gladly obeyed, moving steadilv onward when every step on meant a step toward the end. And in their prostrate forms I read anew the lesson that the soul of this people, which could lift men to such heights, is still a living, moving, flaming thing. And when the evil is measured and the good is counted, I find that the balance is right, and I have faith.

I consider our neighbor nations, each with its glory, each with its gift, each with its task nobly done and its tasks yet to do, its soul too a living, moving, flaming thing. I see again that field of struggle—khaki of Belgium and England, Italy's gray, sky-blue of France, gray-green—yes, gray-green too of enemy dead—little tangled heaps, sleeping together, equal in death—each, right or mistaken, with his vision, each with his power to follow it straight to the end. And of them all—

When the evil is measured and the good is counted, I find that the balance is right, and I say to you I have faith.

Faith in the beauty and glory of manhood everywhere, that through the ages has gone on achieving and building, gathering knowledge, seeking for wisdom, conquering self, until at last from out of the beast we see coming forth the man, the friend, the brother.

I have faith.

I commend to you that faith as the first article of the true Kiwanian's creed.

HOW TO MAKE AN ANNOUNCEMENT

Making an announcement *may be* one of the *simplest tasks* a speaker has to perform. On the other hand, it *may call for the greatest skill in persuasion.*

Here is a very simple announcement.

BRIEF ANNOUNCEMENT OF A "JUNIOR EXPOSITION" (FICTITIOUS)

(This speech is quoted from a text-book, entitled "Oral English" by John M. Brewer, formerly teacher in the Los Angeles, California, High School. It is quoted because it embodies in brief form the essentials of all announcement speeches.)

"The second annual junior exposition, for the exhibition of the products and interests of the children of this city, will be held on next Friday afternoon and evening. Last year's success is to be repeated on a larger and more comprehensive scale. The section devoted to children's pets has been greatly enlarged, and sections for kites and for home decoration have been added.

"The exposition is to be held in Convention Hall, on Williamson Street, and will be open from three to ten in the afternoon. The admission to everyone is ten cents.

"Remember: Friday next; Convention Hall; three to ten in the afternoon; the Junior Exposition."

Here is a more pretentious announcement.

The following speech is a more fully developed announcement speech, probably representing the extreme opposite of the preceding speech. *The first speech* was reduced to the very lowest terms, and almost approaches billboard *simplicity.* *This* speech is expanded until it assumes *the dignity of a major part in a set program.* Each is suited to its purpose, and anyone asked to make a speech of announcement should consider carefully the importance of the event to be announced to the audience, and should *expand* the bare announcement *to such proportions as are fitting.* If programs of the event are in the hands of the audience, as is the case in the following speech, less emphasis need be laid on the time, place, and conditions of admission. If programs are not in the hands of the audience, these details must be made extremely clear. The tone of the speech differs with the occasion.

When *mere information* is set forth, a clear *statement of the facts is all that is necessary.* When persuasion is sought, the speaker should utilize all the devices that good speaking would call for.

(*Following lessons* in this course will show the beginner *how to persuade* people to do the thing he wants them to do.)

Study the following outline and notice how it is applied in the speech that follows:

SUGGESTIVE OUTLINE FOR THE ANNOUNCEMENT SPEECH

1. State the characteristics of the event to be announced
   (*a*) Its importance
   (*b*) Its object
   (*c*) Of what it will consist
2. Present the general arguments which should make the event of interest to the audience
   (*a*) The reputation of the men who will speak
   (*b*) The importance of the subject discussed
   (*c*) The problems that must be solved.
3. Present the program in detail
   (*a*) The importance of each discussion

   (*b*) The features of recreation, if any
4. Name the conditions of attendance
   (*a*) The price of admission
   (*b*) The time of the event
   (*c*) The place of the event
   (*d*) Whether membership of any sort if necessary
5. Present an optimistic view of what the event will be or will accomplish
6. Appeal to those present to attend

ANNOUNCING A CONGRESS ON INLAND WATERWAYS

By William H. Adams

Chairman of the Committee on Inland Waterways, Detroit Board of Commerce

(Speech delivered before the Exchange Club, Detroit, Michigan, at a luncheon.)

There will be held this week in Detroit a history-making conference toward which the eyes of the entire West are looking. Most great men are not appreciated in their own home town, at least not until the outside world has acknowledged their greatness, and it may be the case with us here in Detroit that we do not appreciate the tremendous significance of this movement to make ocean ports out of the Great Lakes cities. This movement is rapidly gathering strength and the first great meeting of the advocates of this improvement is to be held here in our own city the last three days of this week. To this meeting will come many of the truly great men of transportation, of commerce, and of business, men who have set their hands to this enterprise—to bring the Atlantic to the heart of the continent—as the one great and necessary thing to be done in this generation.

Not every generation has its great problems to solve. The generation of pioneers who built the tremendous railroad system of the middle west and loom up like giants in the commercial history of our country has passed away. For the many years since that day the transportation facilities of our country have simply marked time and while business has doubled and tripled in magnitude, railroads have actually decreased in mileage, rolling stock has gone to the scrap heap and has not been replaced and costly terminals so badly needed have been planned but their construction has been continually delayed. The time has come for the next great epoch in the transportation history of our country and we of this day and this city are privileged to have a hand in initiating and driving to completion the great enterprise which will bring ocean navigation to our very doors and relieve us for all time of the destructive embargoes which threaten our industrial life.

The project to create from the Great Lakes an American Mediterranean is not new. Four hundred years ago Marquette and LaSalle foresaw the day when this inland empire would be in direct touch by water with the Old World. Fifty years ago canals then deemed adequate were built by Canada to by-pass the rapids of the St. Lawrence River and the Falls at Niagara. These canals were scarcely built, however, when a great change took place in the shipping industry of the world. Due to the introduction of steel in ship-building it became practicable to construct and operate ships of much greater size than had before been possible and as result the commercial ocean ship of even thirty years ago had outgrown the St. Lawrence and Welland canals.

There is a popular misconception as to the great size of ocean cargo carriers. The great *Leviathan* makes a good newspaper story but the fact remains that the great tonnage of the world is not in 30,000 ton ships but in ships of less than 5,000 tons. Careful records kept by the United States Shipping Board show that for runs up to 5,000 miles a 6,000 ton ship has a less cost per ton mile than any other size. Eighty-six per cent of all the ships that sail on salt seas could safely and economically navigate the channels which now exist in our Great Lakes and harbors, if it were not for the short stretch of tumbling rapids which obstruct the outlets to the Great Lakes.

The Canadian Government has under construction at this time an enlarged ship canal between Lake Erie and Lake Ontario. This canal is about forty per cent complete and will cost approximately $75,000,000. When in service it will take ships drawing 25 feet of water and with a length of 800 feet and can be easily made to take ships of a draft of 30 feet when lake channels and traffic warrant.

There remains the improvement of the International River which separates and yet connects the United States and her sister nation, Canada.

There formerly existed another barrier in the mutual distrust and suspicion which the two nations had for each other. But a hundred years of peaceful settlement of all kinds of boundary disputes evolved the International Joint Commission to which all matters affecting the two countries are now referred. It remained, however, for the Great War for human liberty to finally bind the two nations with a deep knowledge of each other's integrity, so that without fear of each other, the great resources common to both countries may now be developed.

The marked break down in rail transportation of recent months and years has demonstrated with great thoroughness the extent to which rail transportation facilities have been neglected and allowed to run down. I do not need to illustrate to convince you of these facts. Every one of you who is at all connected with commercial life is keenly alive to the situation today. A few examples will suffice.

Mr. W. L. Ross, President of the Cloverleaf Railroad, at the hearing before the International Joint Commission in Toledo in June stated that there had been at times held in Toledo as many as 7,000 carloads of merchandise destined to Atlantic seaports which could not be handed over to the railroads running east from Toledo because of embargoes against seaboard districts. This virtually means that every siding east of

Toledo was clogged with loaded cars. It was further stated at this hearing that it commonly takes from 70 to 90 days for a carload of Toledo-produced merchandise to be placed alongside ocean cargo carriers for export.

Indeed it seems hopeless to expect in the future, any such conditions as once obtained in railroad operation. With the greatly increased cost of right of way and rolling stock, it is becoming increasingly impossible for railroads to finance their operations and in many of our cities and in Detroit particularly the additional cost of improved terminal facilities and particularly land is almost prohibitive.

The one relief possible is the waterway. Here there are no side tracks to become congested and endless streams of ships in both directions can traverse safely the same broad track. The lakes to ocean waterway will virtually form a belt line around the congested eastern district of our country. Coastwise trade goods can be delivered to Manhattan Island in not to exceed fourteen days and at a cost far less than by rail.

The "street" estimates that the railroads will shortly be allowed to increase freight rates varying from twenty-five per cent to fifty per cent. Whatever figure is finally used it is certain that the increase will be very radical. The first class freight rate to New York is now in excess of $20 per ton with a possibility of $30 per ton. Is it not about time that the possibilities of the all-water route shall be studied?

With the knowledge of these matters a^ the powerful motive the Board of Commerce of Detroit with the Great Lakes St. Lawrence Tidewater Association has arranged a great Convention or Congress to be held in the auditorium of the Board of Commerce, Thursday, Friday and Saturday of this week. You have before you the program. Mr. Gardner who is a banker and business man of Chicago will at the first session outline the work which has been done up to date. Senator Townsend of Michigan will give the national aspects of the case. In the evening session, Mr. Charles K. Anderson will discuss the proposed improvement from the standpoint of the great manufacturing interests of the country. Mr. Anderson believes that New York manufacturers and commercial interests will strongly indorse this enterprise when they realize the quick and relatively cheap connection which New York will have with the middle west by means of this improved waterway.

In the evening at a dinner meeting, Senator Lenroot will show us the rising tide of public sentiment in the west which demands the natural outlet to the sea. Dr. MacElwee will make clear to us how we are hampered in our business by inadequate terminals and how our costs are affected by our present day methods of transfer. This will be an illustrated lecture.

On Friday General Beach will discuss the physical problems involved and Gardner S. Williams of Ann Arbor will discuss the tremendous value of the power which will be developed in connection with the river improvement. I will not take your time to read over the rest of the program with you. I can assure you that the men who will discuss the various phases of this work are among the strongest men of our country and they are all united in urging the immediate construction of the St. Lawrence improvement as a national necessity for this vast inland empire.

It is obvious that industrial Detroit has a tremendous interest in this project. The export business of Detroit is already large, but it all pays toll to Atlantic seaports and the time lost in rail transit is frequently costly and annoying. Goods are out of date before they can be delivered to the buyer and it is impossible to set a delivery date, thus making it almost impossible to do business with certain classes of foreign trade. When we have regular ship sailings from Detroit we can give with certainty arrival dates when our foreign customers may expect to receive their goods. The rail and ocean freight rate from Detroit to European ports is now more than $50 per ton. Thirty dollars per ton of this cost should be saved and when competition is restored in world trade as it will then do before many years elapse a $30 per ton handicap will be a very serious matter. How can Detroit manufacturers compete in the markets of the world with such a differential? When that day of competition comes we must have our waterway ready for use.

The International Joint Commission to which this matter has been referred is obliged to make its final report not later than December of this year. It will then be up to Congress and the Canadian Parliament to appropriate a revolving fund for the construction of this improvement, which will be later repaid from the proceeds of power for which there is so much demand throughout New York and New England. We shall need the strong backing of enlightened public opinion when Congress is in session and I urge every man of you who believes in his own future and his business to attend the sessions of the Congress of this week and become informed concerning the various phases of this important question. If possible register as delegates and attend all sessions. You need not be members of the Board of Commerce but all business men and women will be welcomed. We are expecting about one thousand delegates from outside of Detroit and we believe that Detroit business men will not be less interested than the men of Portland, Spokane and Chicago.

ASSIGNMENT:

Twelve kinds of speeches have really been dealt with in this lesson. They are: The speech presenting a personal gift to a friend before a small group of mutual friends; the speech presenting a gift to an individual (not an intimate personal friend) before a small group of acquaintances (such as would be found in a committee that has been working together over a period of time); the speech presenting a personal gift to an officer of an organization, before the members of that organization; the speech presenting a memorial gift to an institution or organization; the speech presenting a practical gift (not a memorial) to an organization or institution; the speech *accepting* a personal gift before a small group of friends; the speech *accepting* a personal gift before a group such as a committee; the speech *accepting* a personal gift before a *large group,* such as an organization, a club, the employees of a business firm; the speech *accepting an office,* immediately upon being elected to that office; the speech of *inauguration;* the short speech of *announcement* for the purpose of *mere information;* the *extended speech of announcement* for the purpose of *persuasion.*

As the subject of your *second prepared speech* choose one of these kinds of speeches, any particular one that may appeal strongly to you and which you think you can handle well.

After first *carefully thinking out* your speech, MAKE A GOOD OUTLINE and prepare your notes in good form (if you use notes).

Do not fail to rehearse the finished *speech once or twice.*

Keep a *REAL SITUATION* in mind.

NOTE: There are many good books on the market giving examples of speeches for special occasions.

The following books are especially good:

Modern Short Speeches, O'Neill,
The Century Co., N. Y.

Models of Speech Composition, O'Neill,
The Century Co., N. Y.

Modern Speeches, Lindgren, F. A.
Crofts Co., N. Y.

Public Speaking for Business Men, Hoffman,
McGraw-Hill Book Co., N. Y.

I presume some of these books are in your public library. If not, *did you know almost any public library will buy any book you ask them to?!*

N.B. *This note alone is worth the price of this course* to any speaker who did not know of these books, or of the general policy of libraries in regard to the purchase of books.